Enchanted
COLOR BY NUMBERS

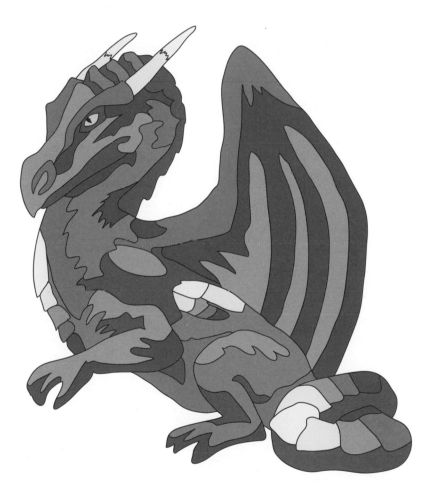

ARCTURUS

ARCTURUS

This edition published in 2022 by Arcturus Publishing Limited
26/27 Bickels Yard, 151–153 Bermondsey Street,
London SE1 3HA

Copyright © Arcturus Holdings Limited

Illustrations: Andres Vaisberg with Diego Vaisberg, DGPH Design and Visual Arts Studio
Design: Tania Field
Editorial Manager: Joe Harris
Design Manager: Jessica Holliland

ISBN: 978-1-3988-1963-4
CH010337NT
Supplier 29, Date 0322, PI 00001066

Printed in China

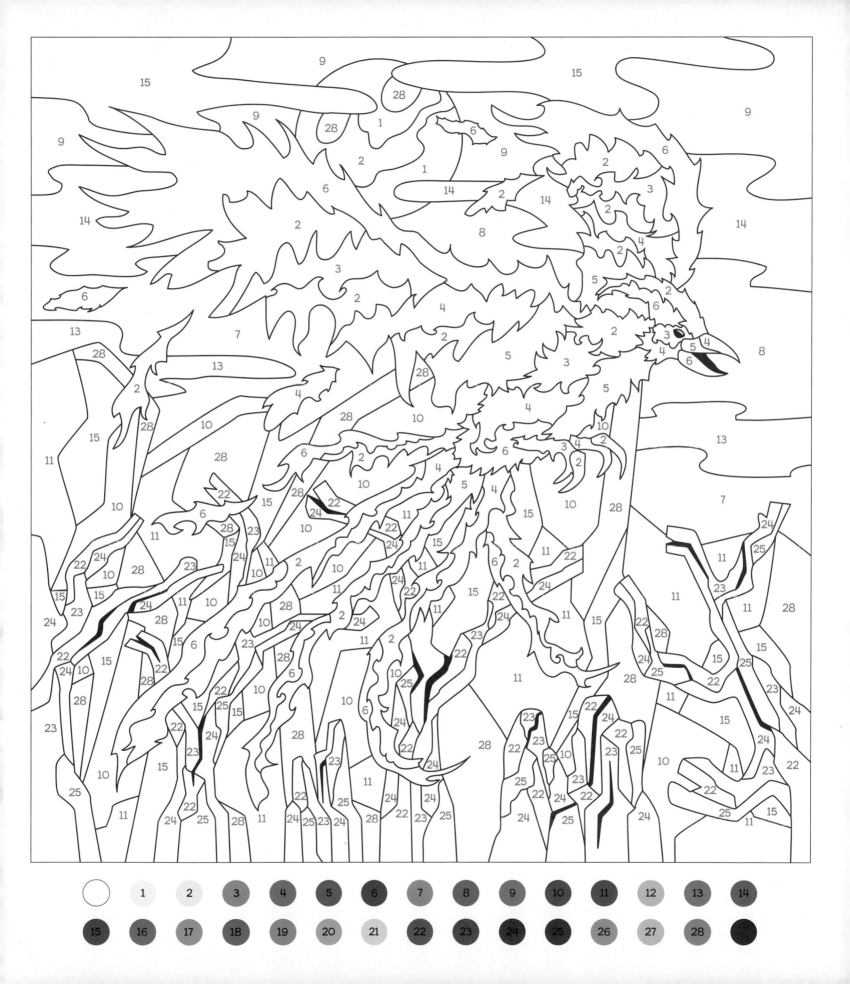

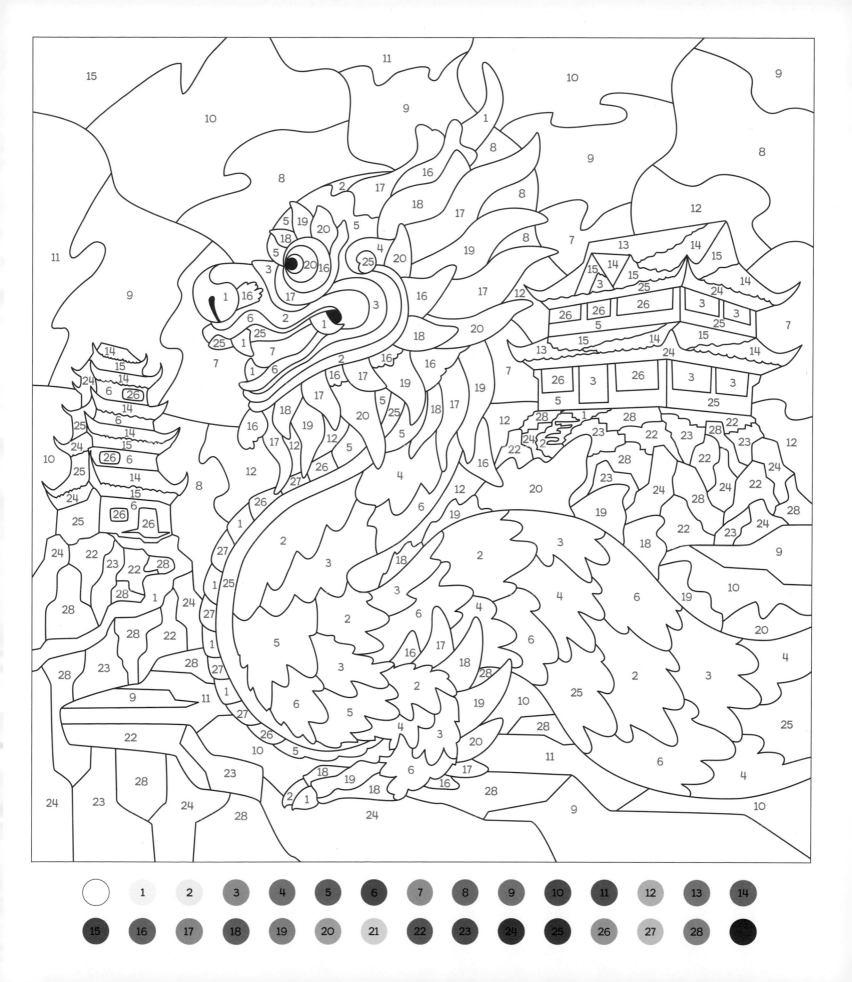

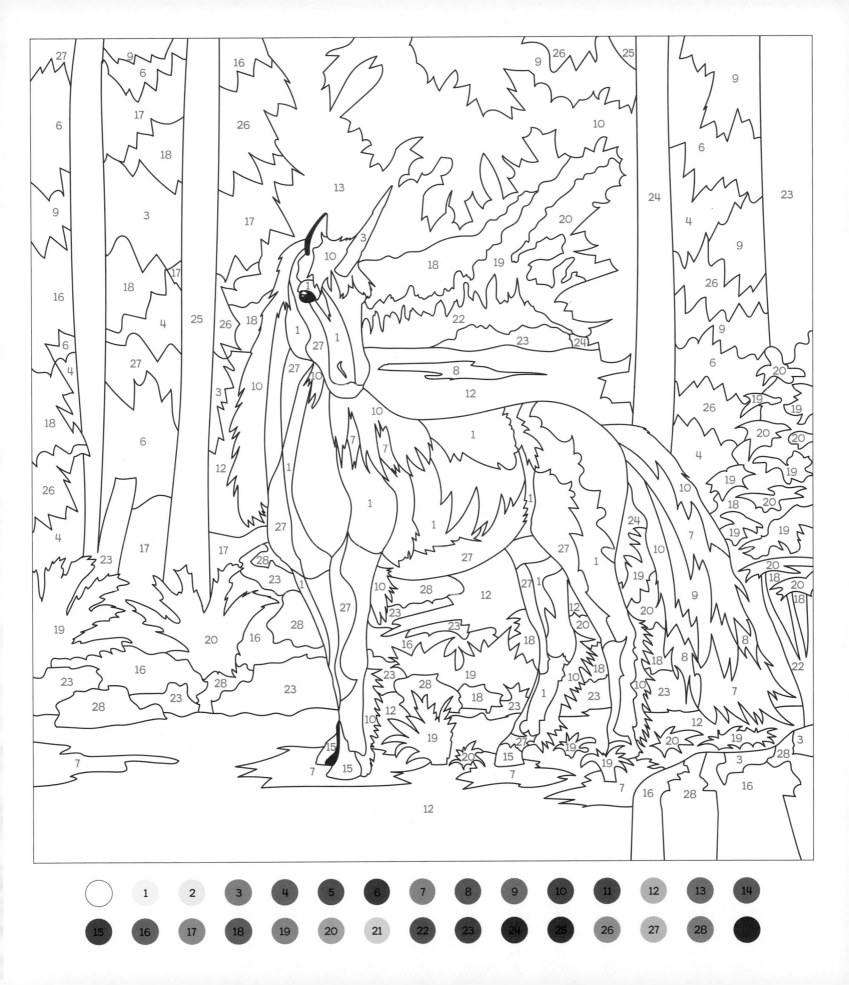

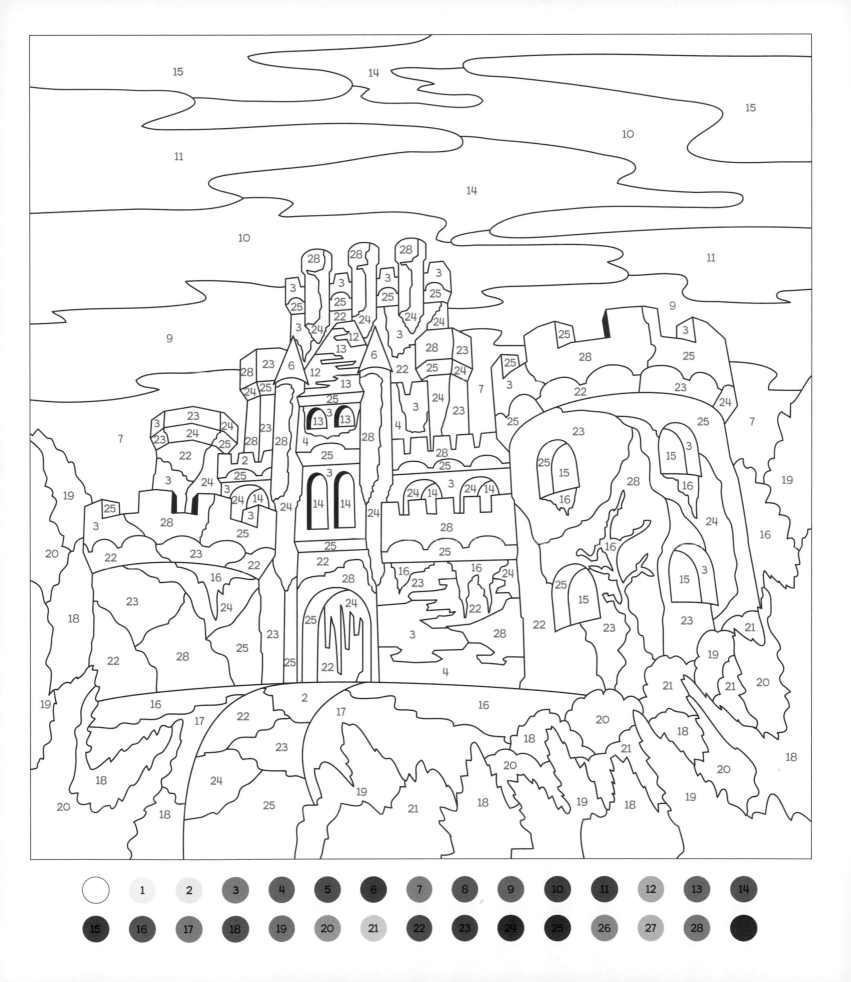

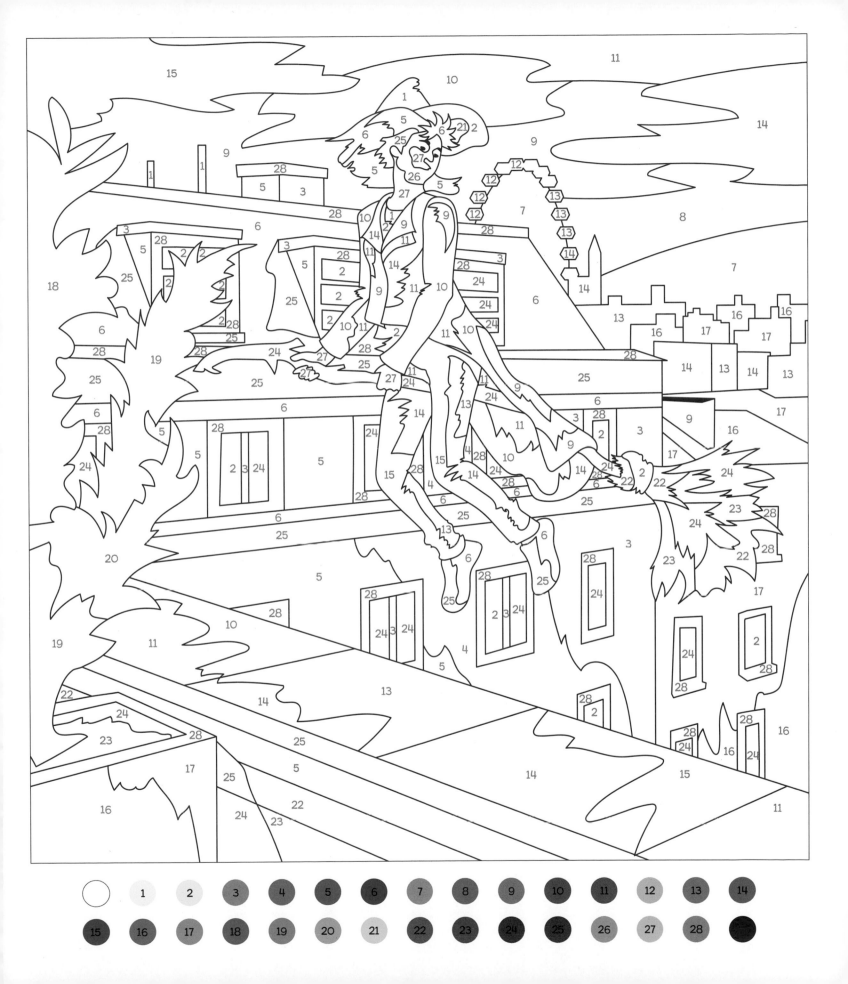

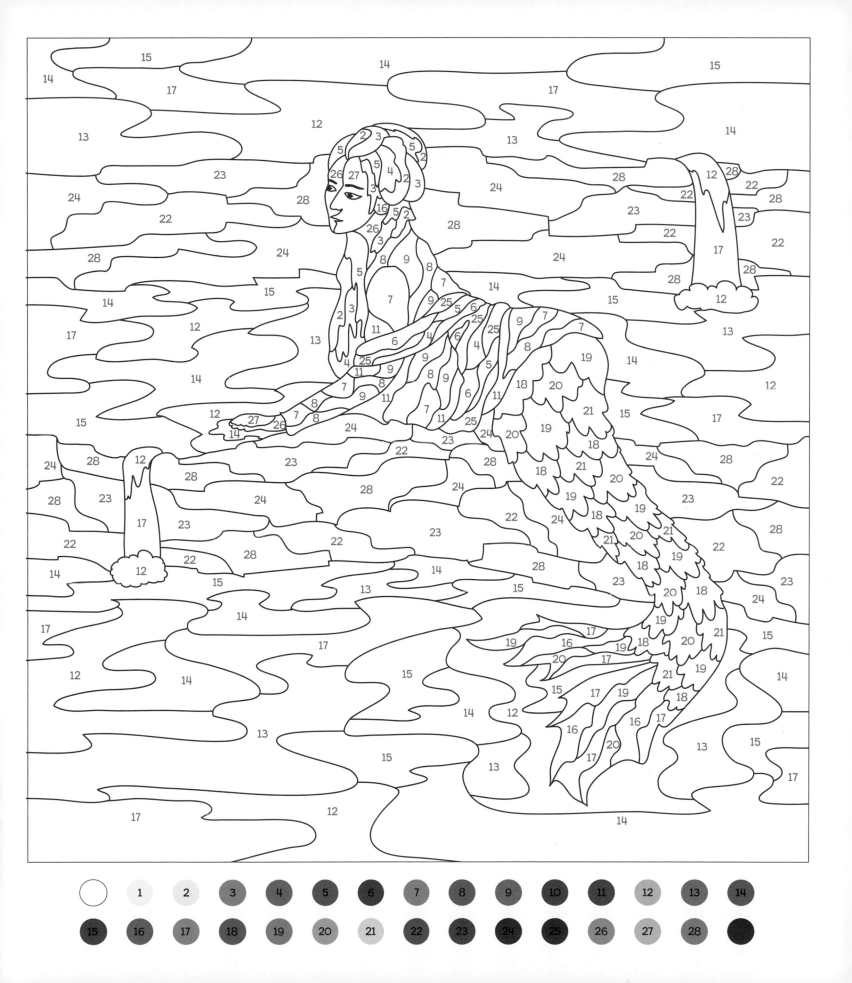

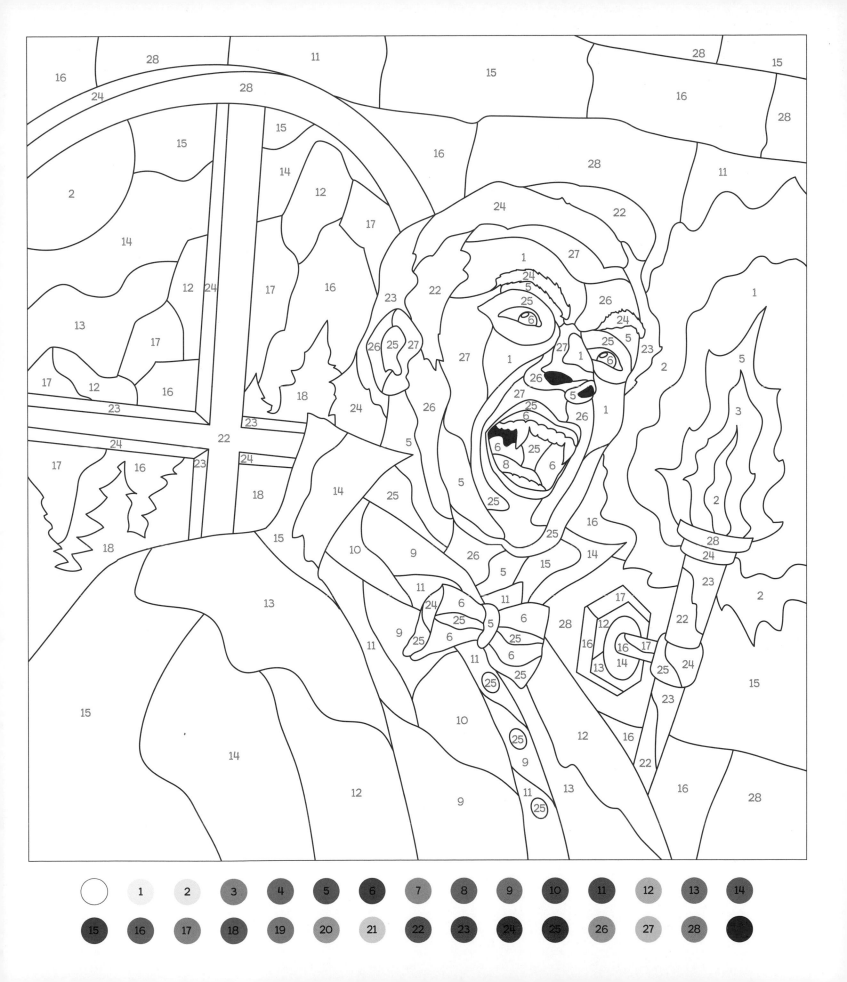

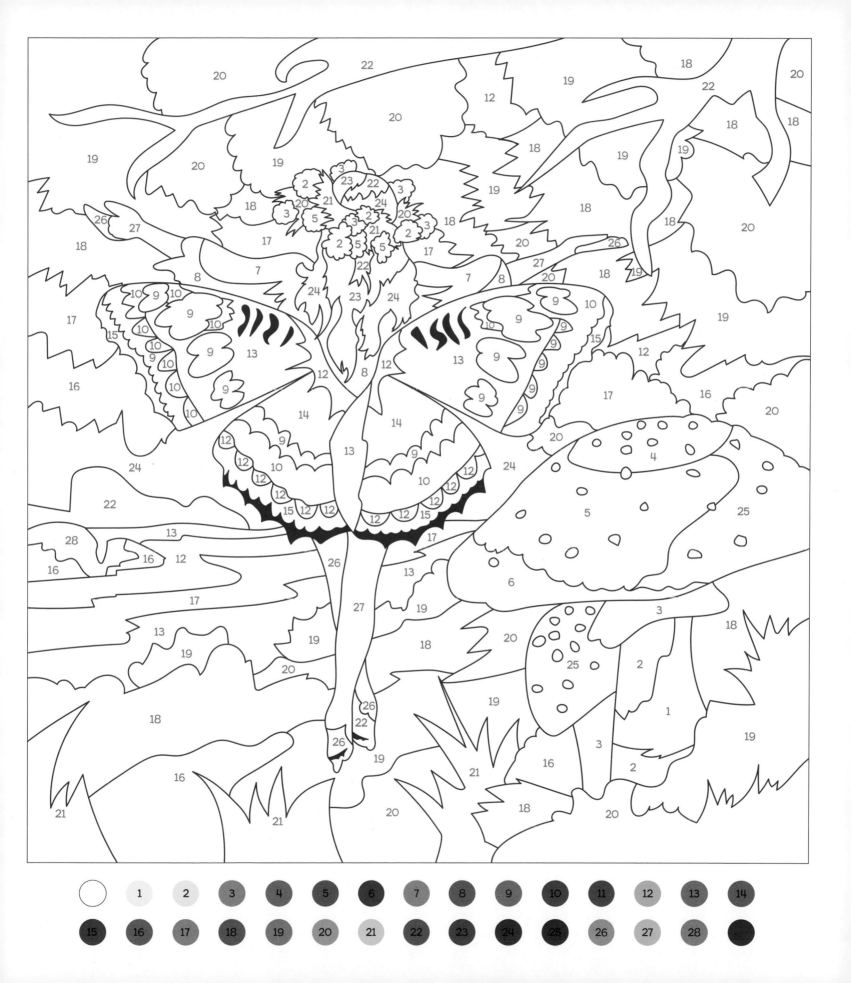

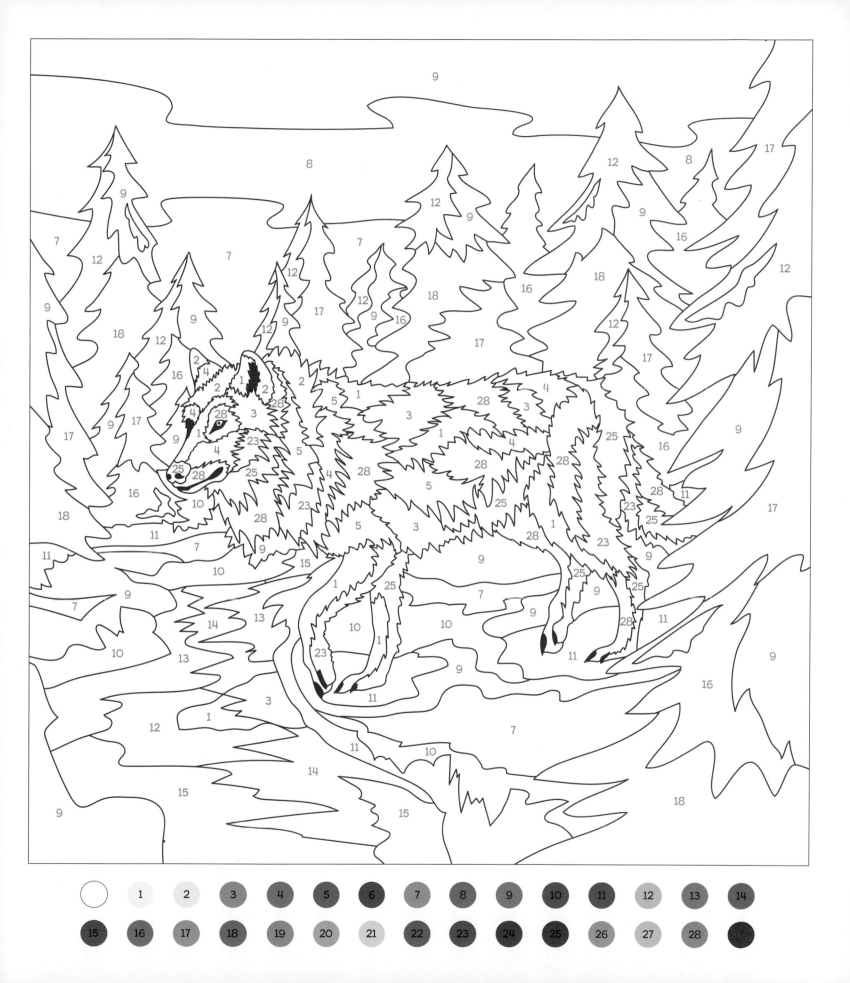

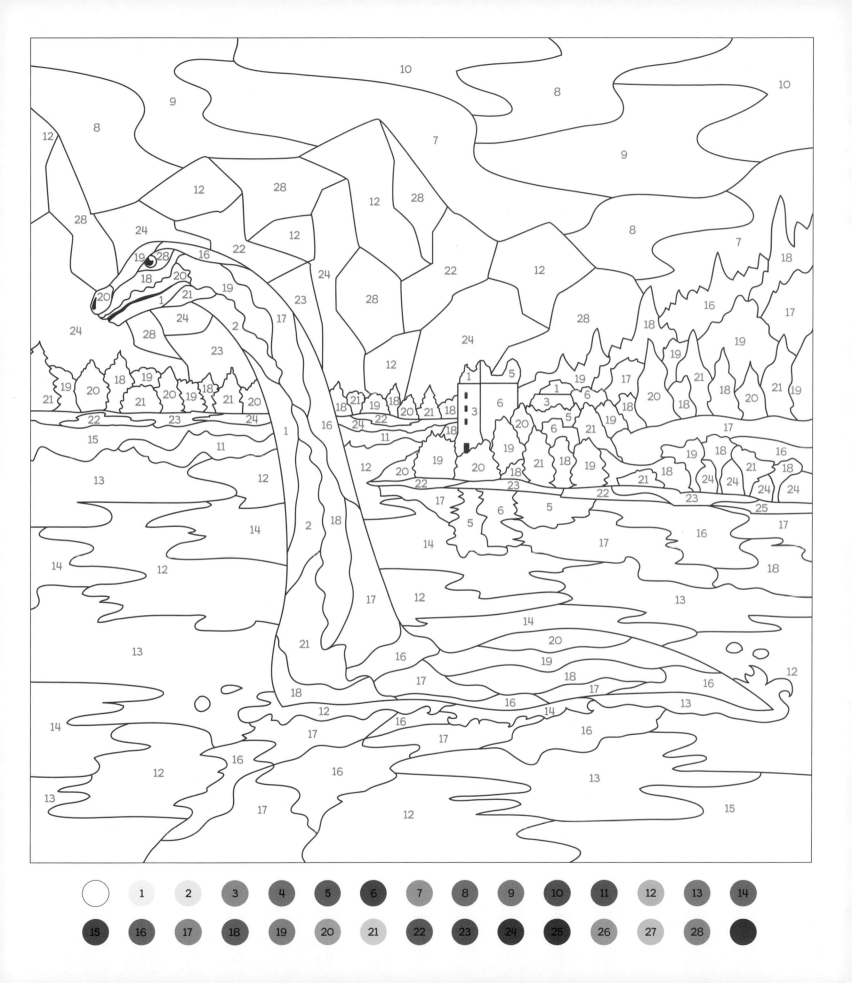

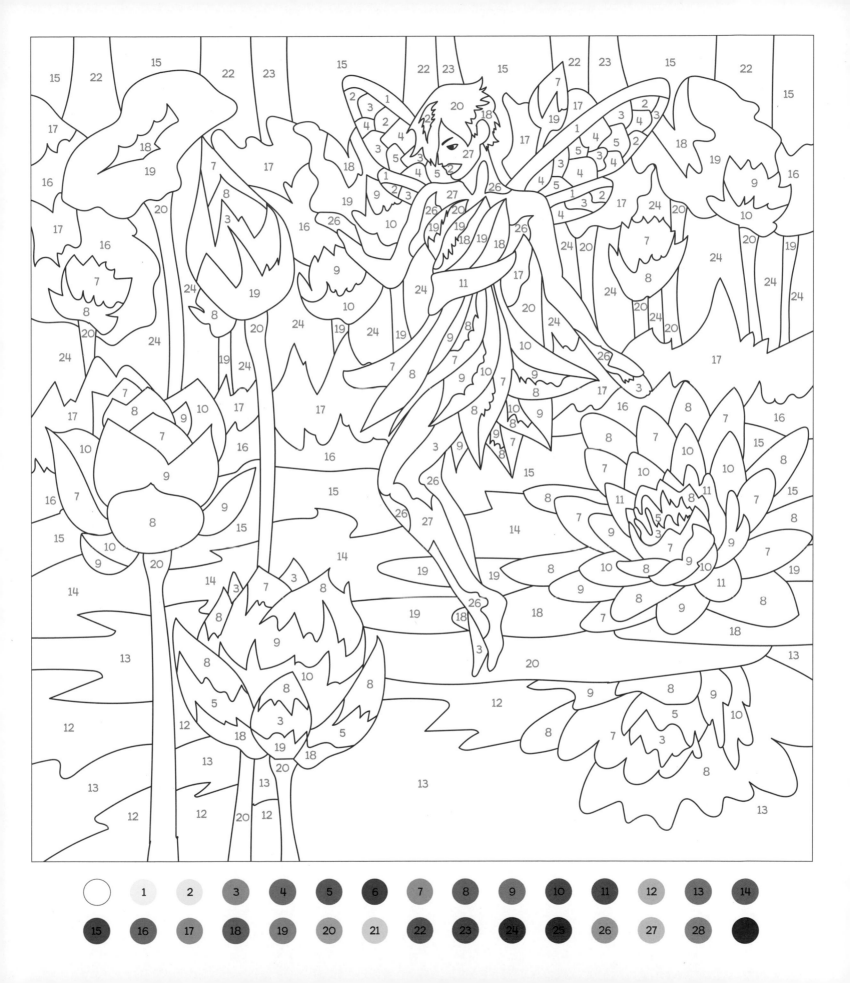

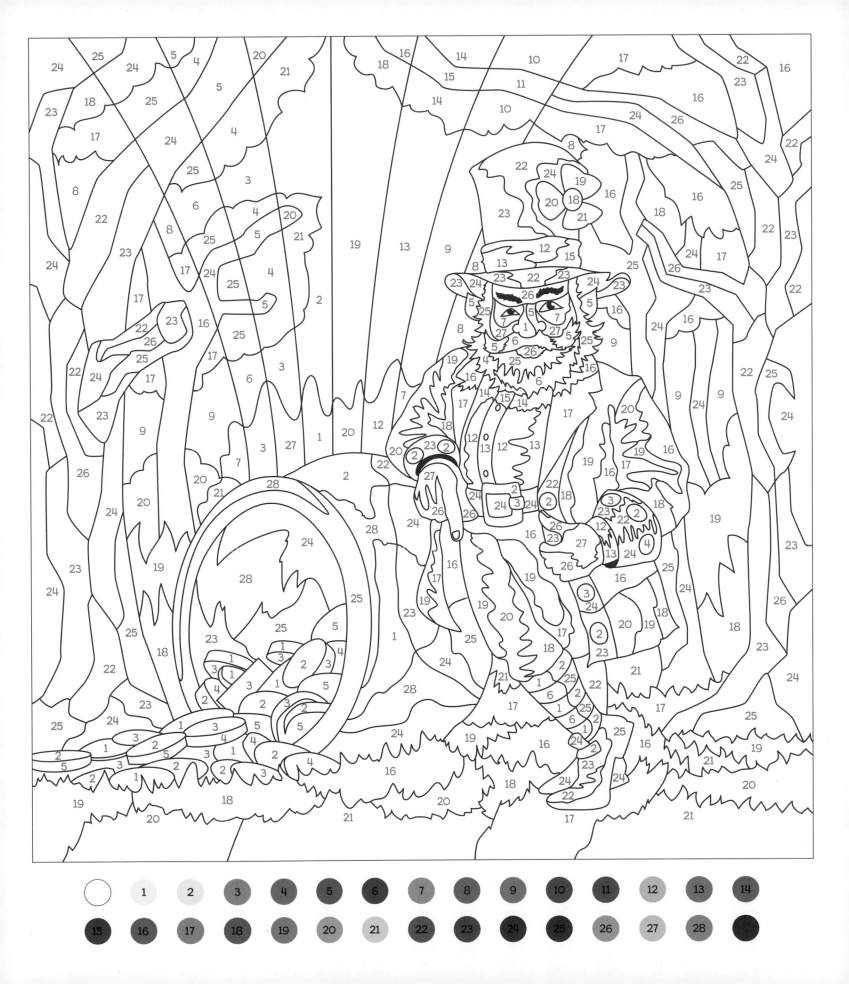

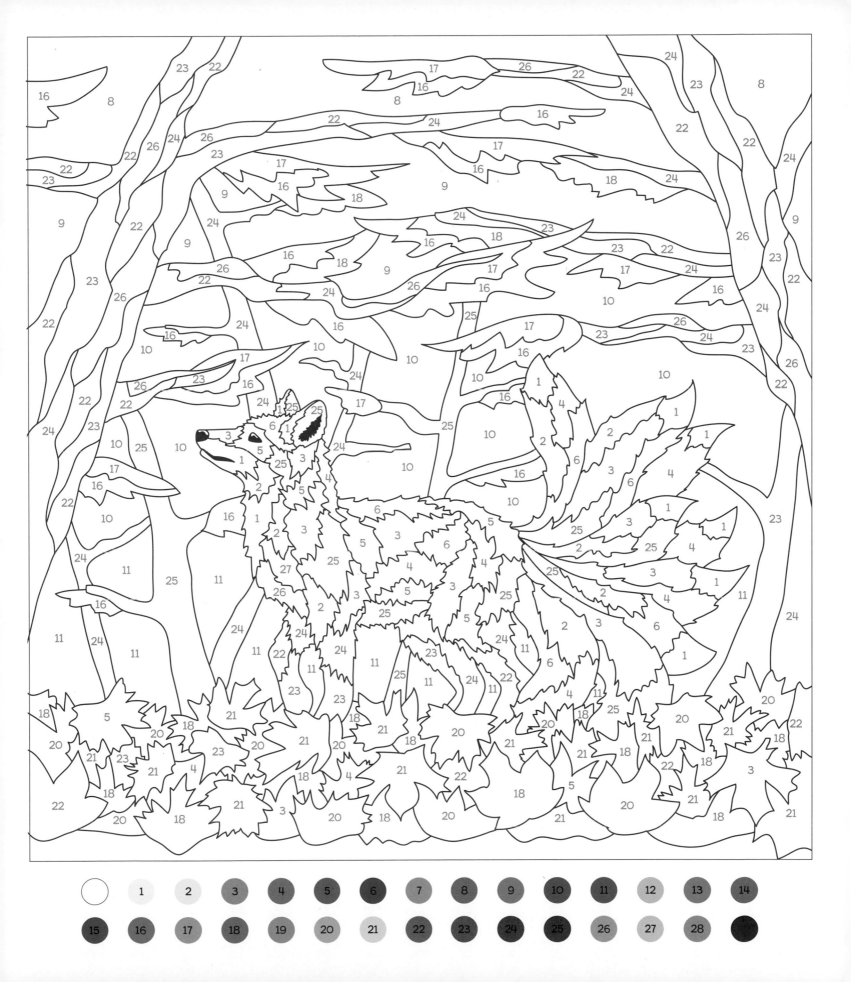

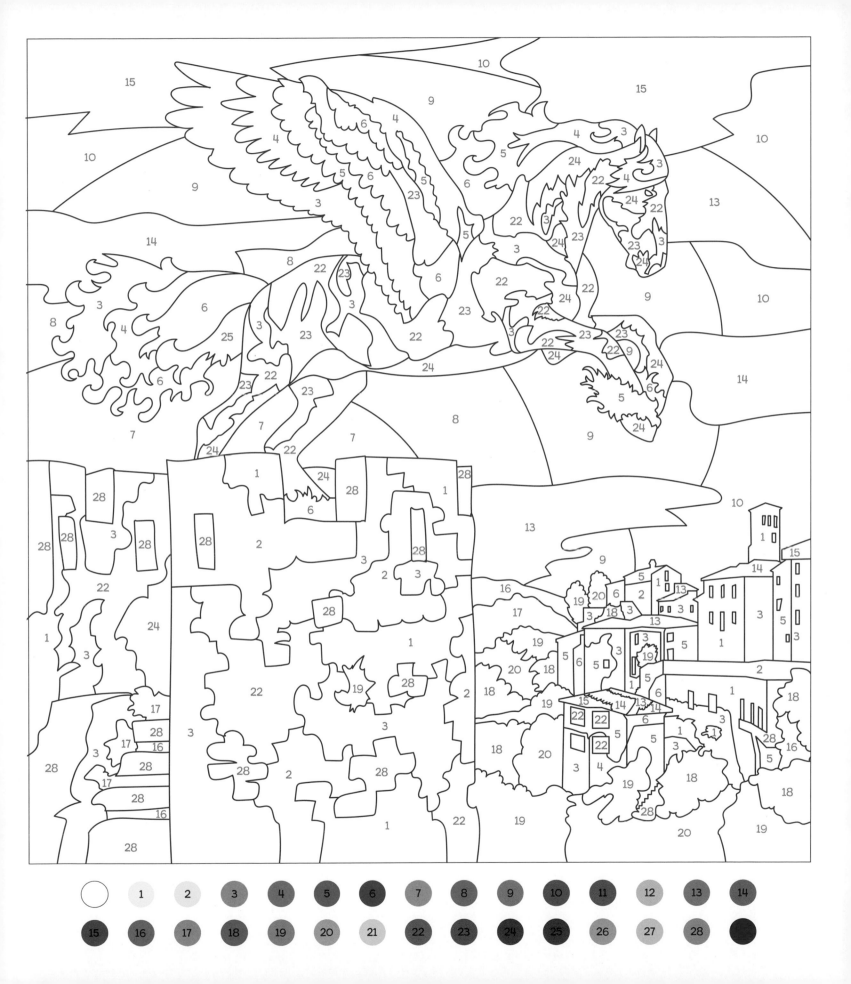

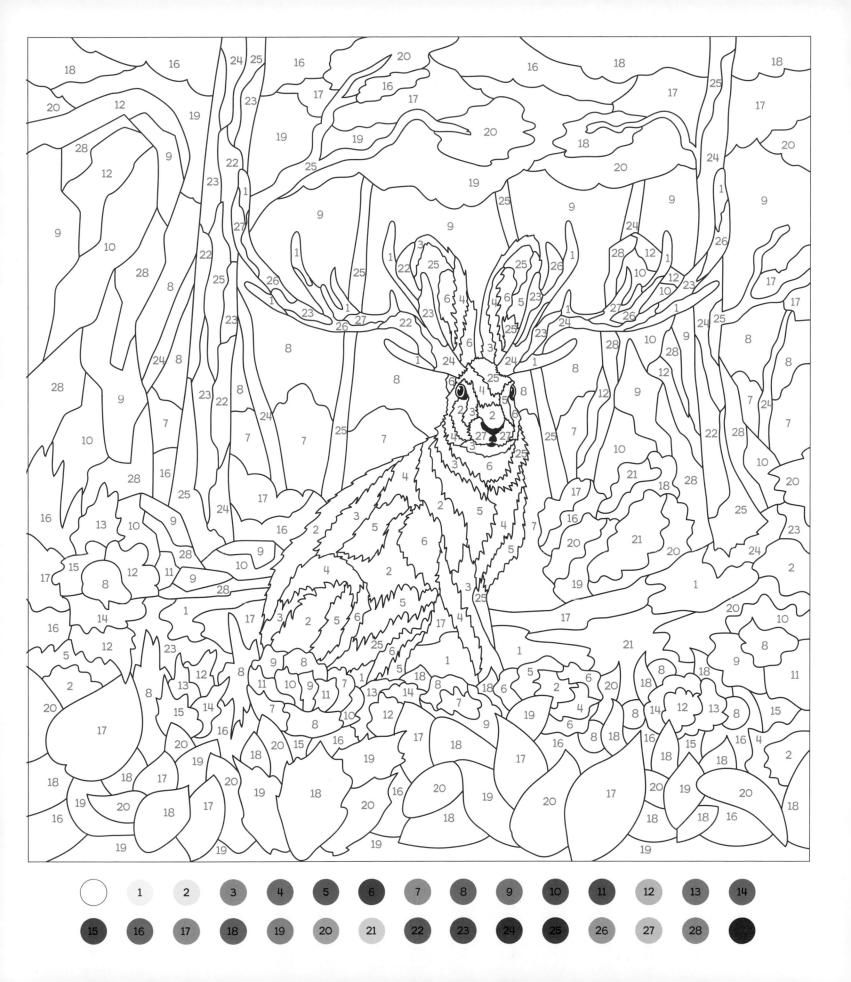

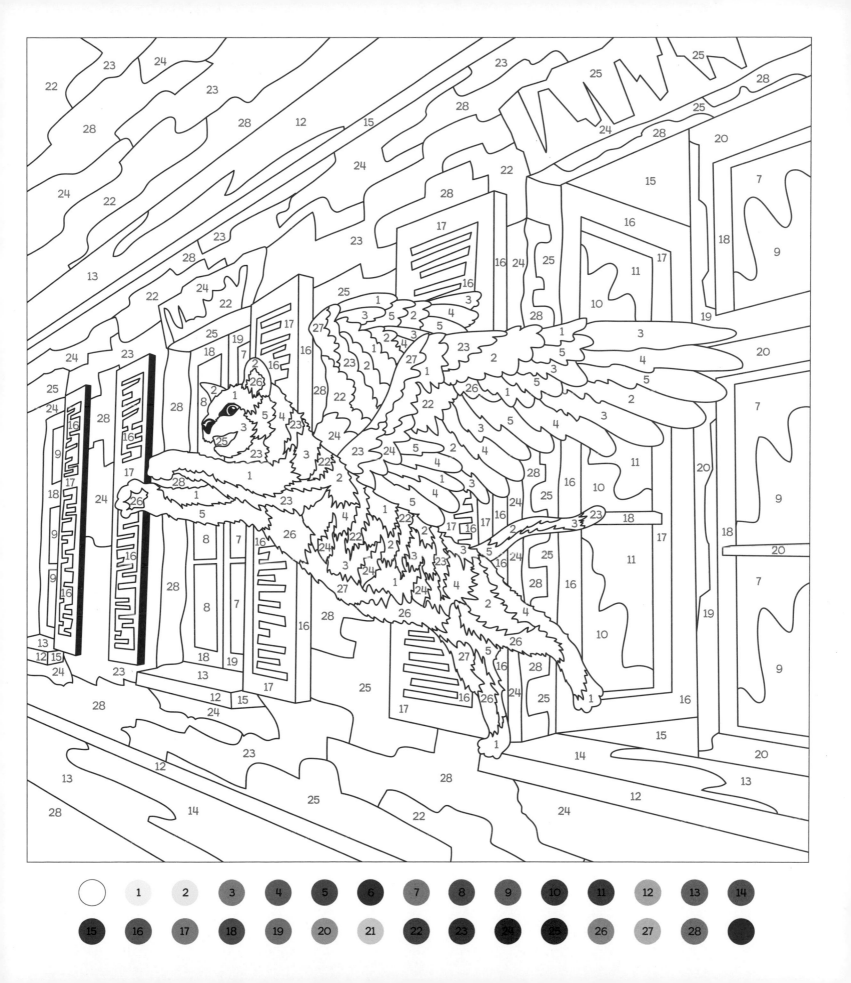

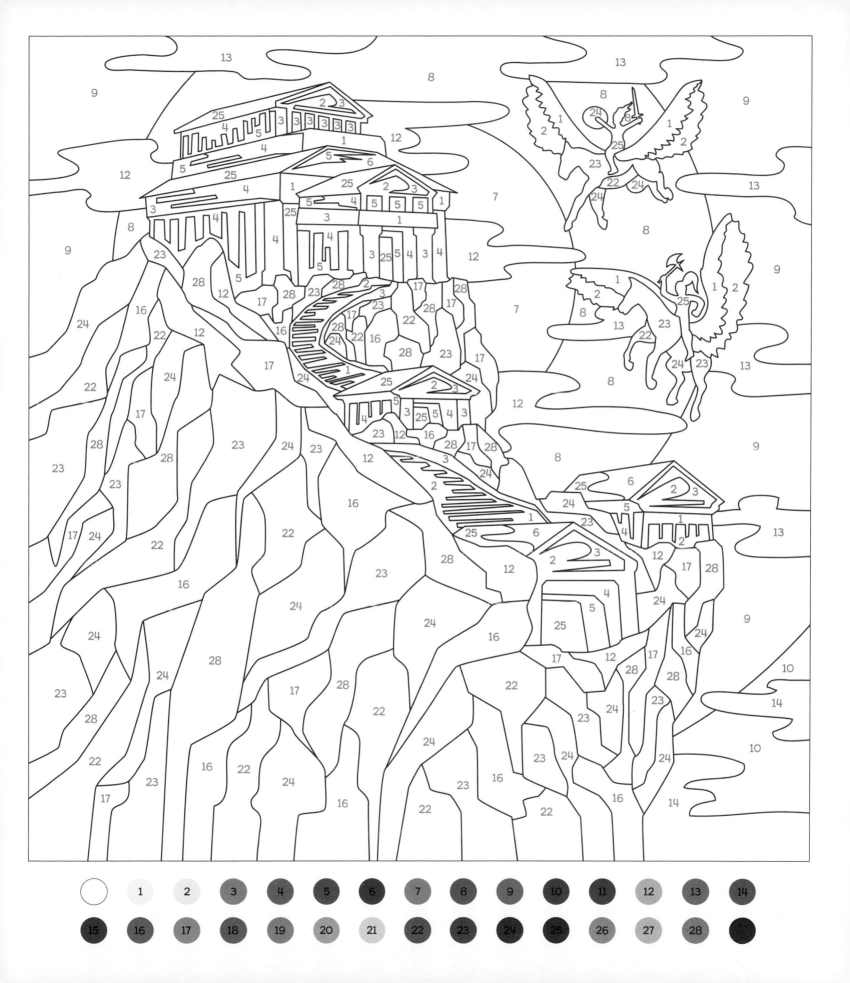

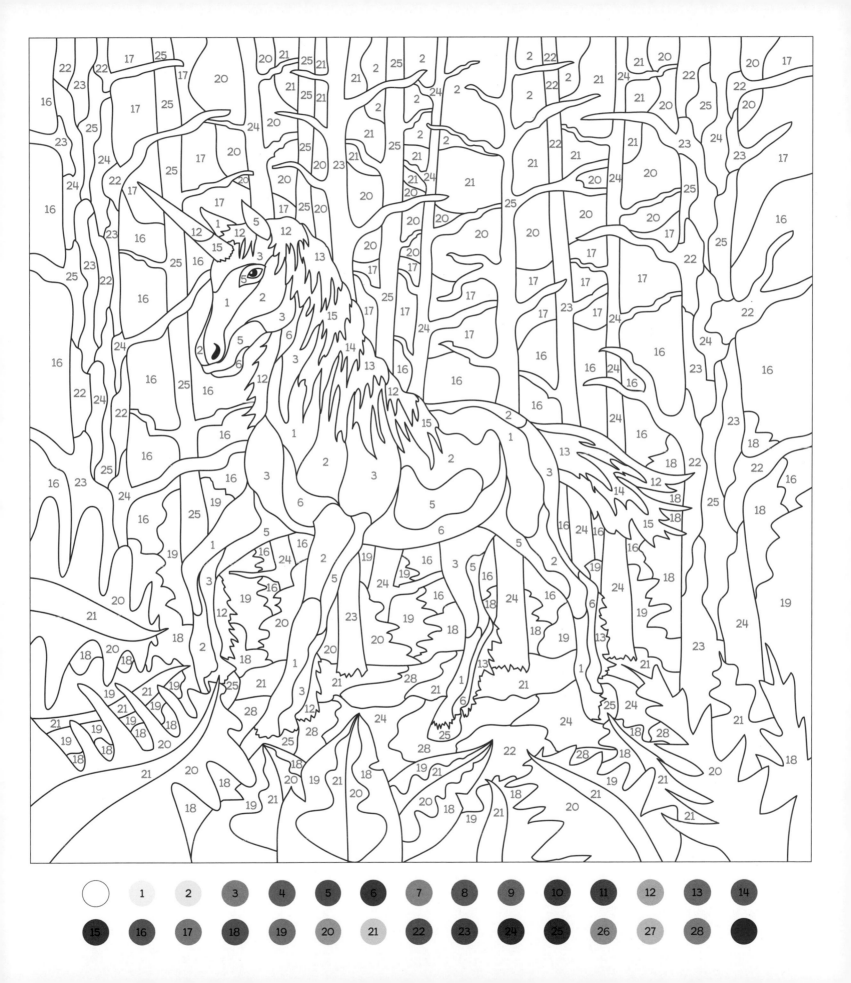

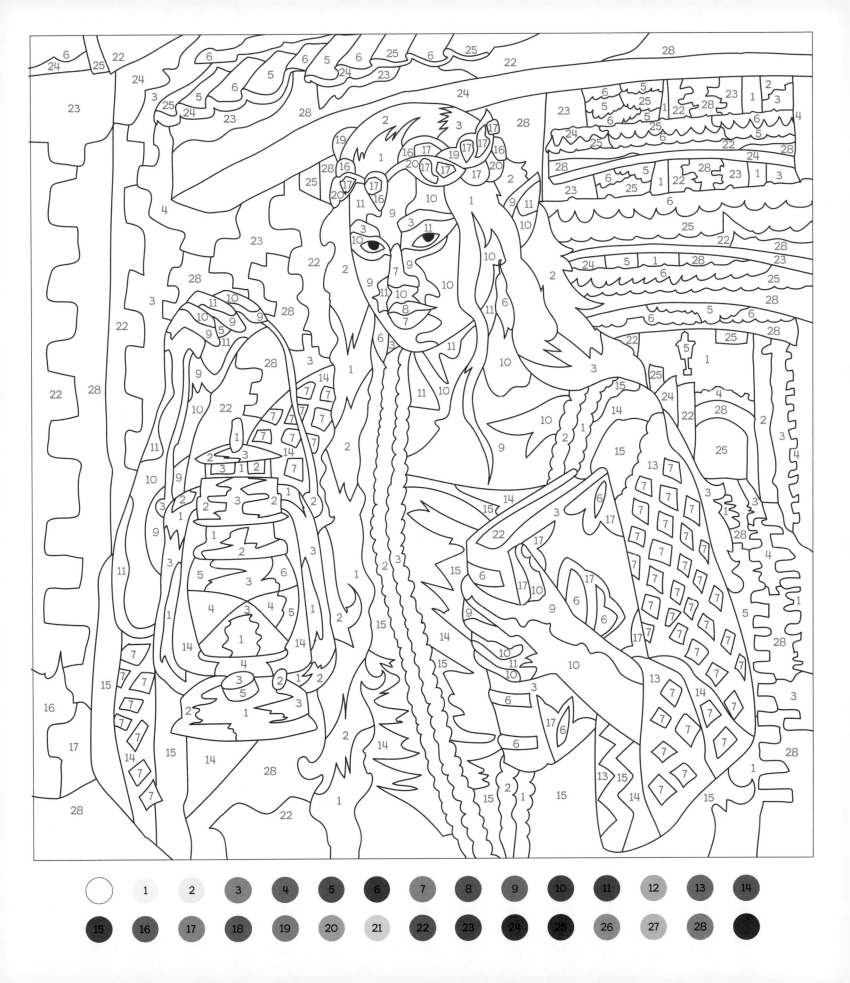

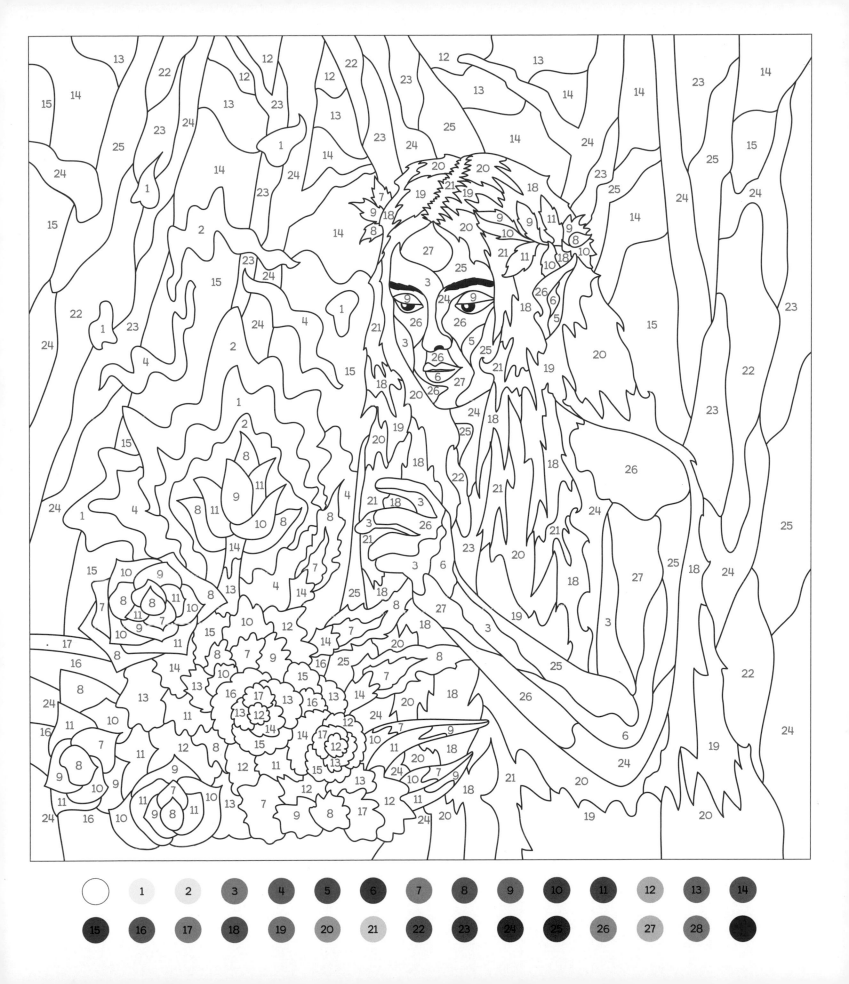

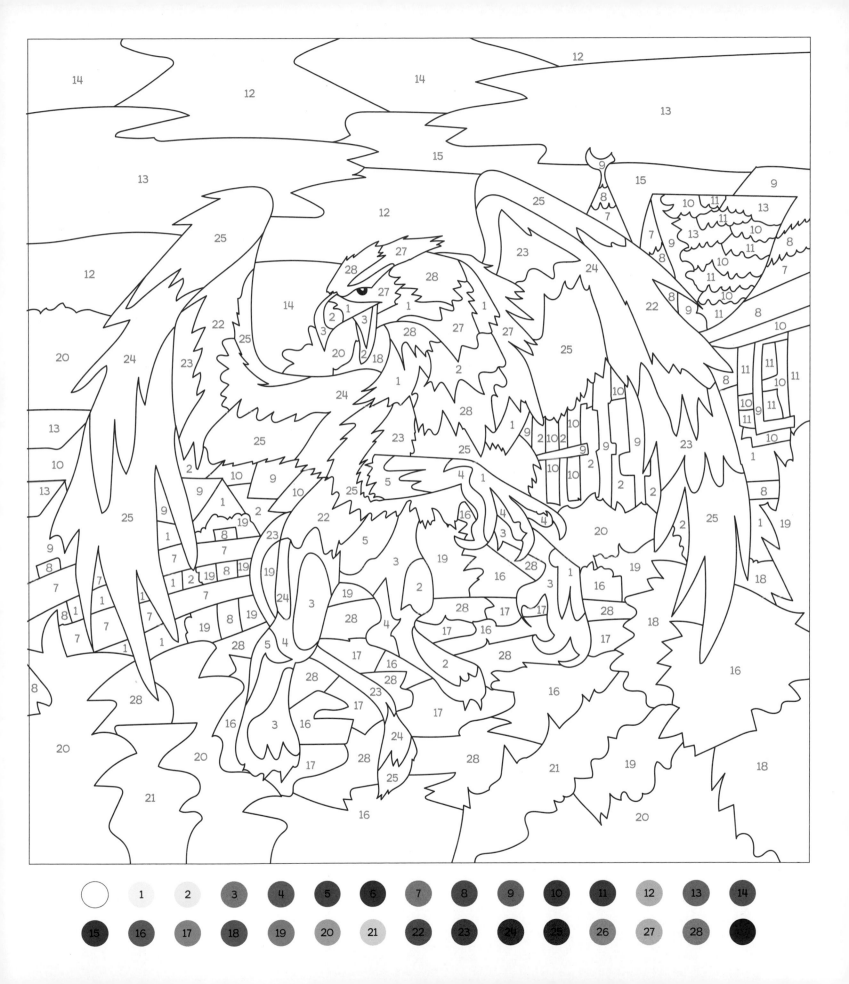

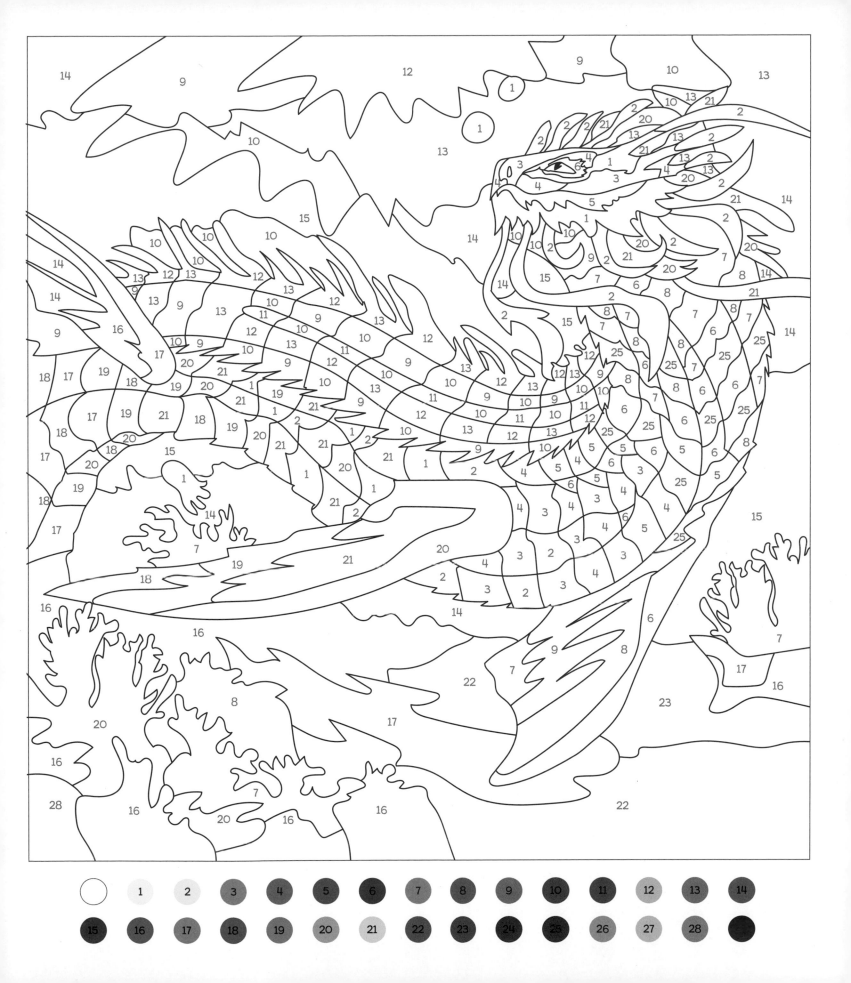

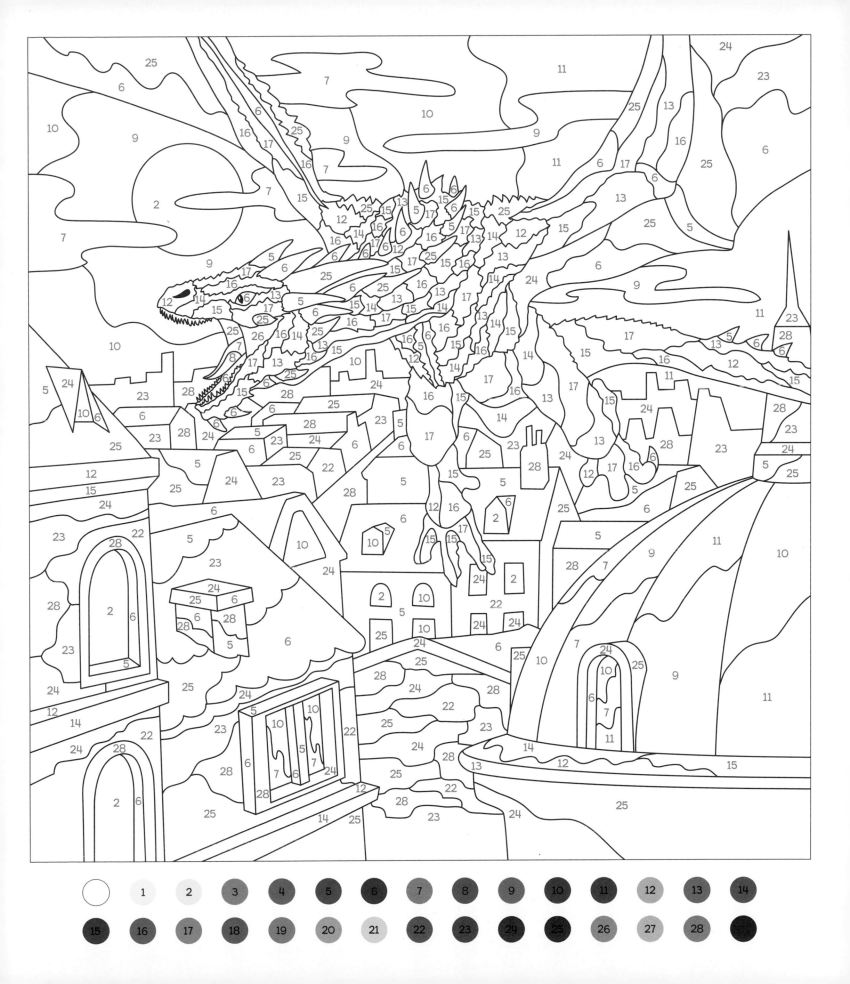

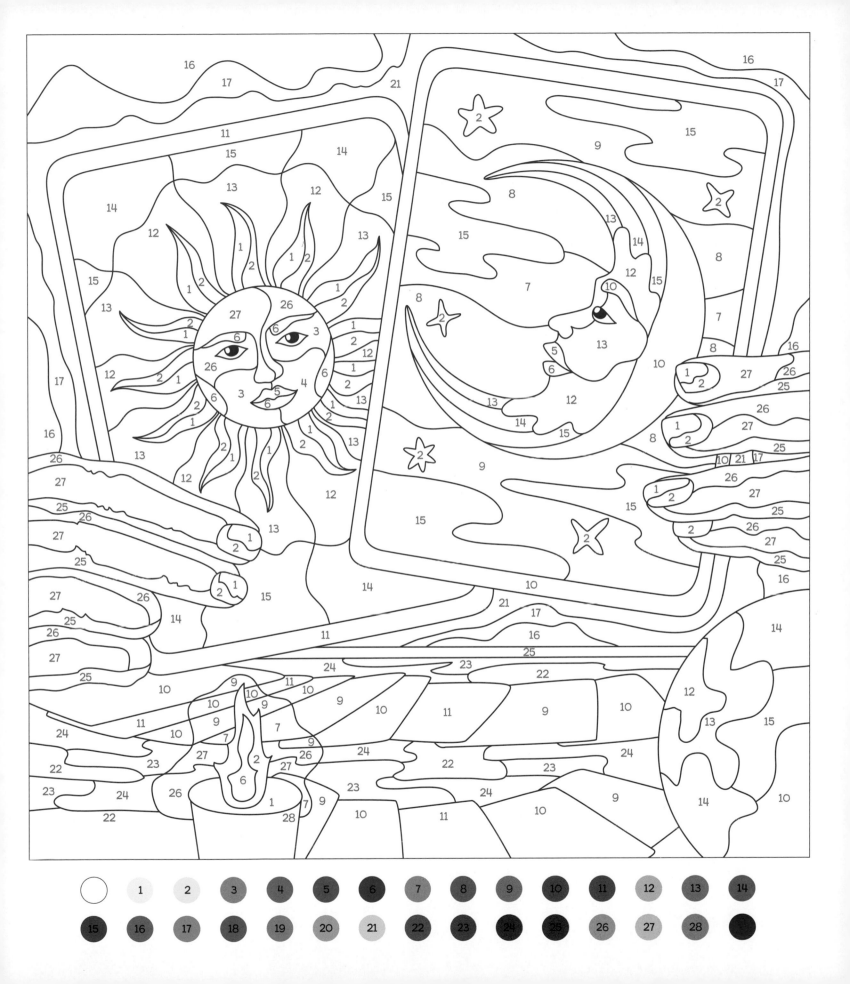

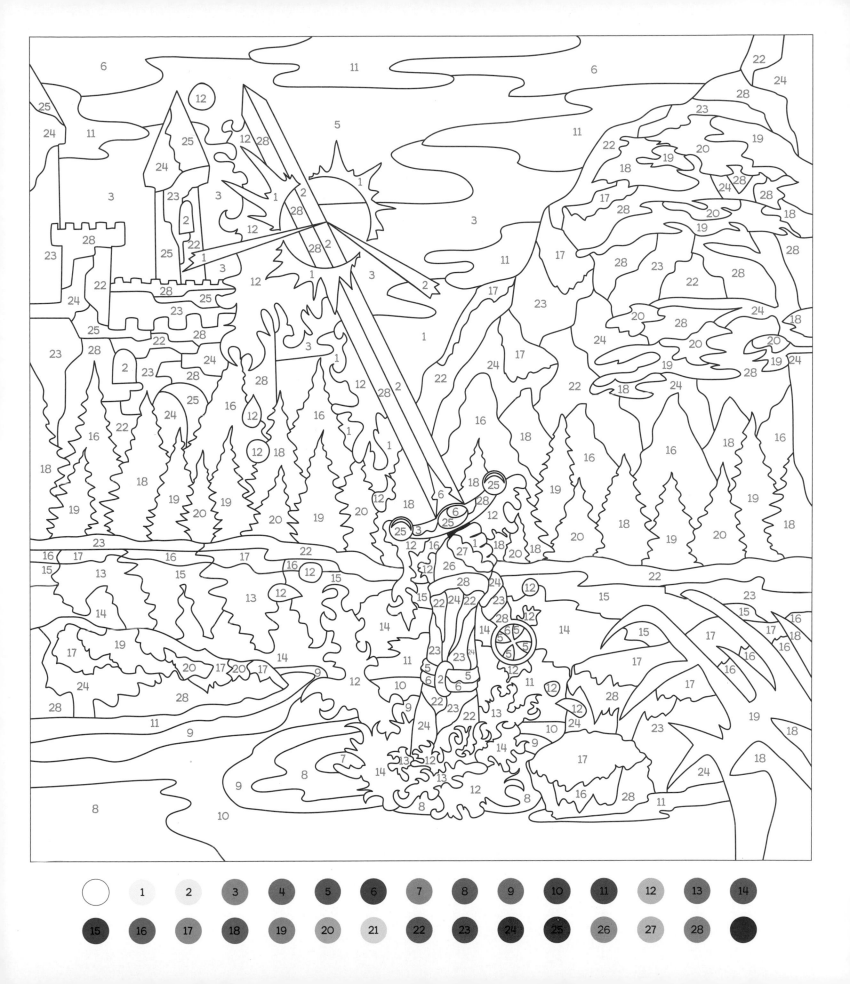

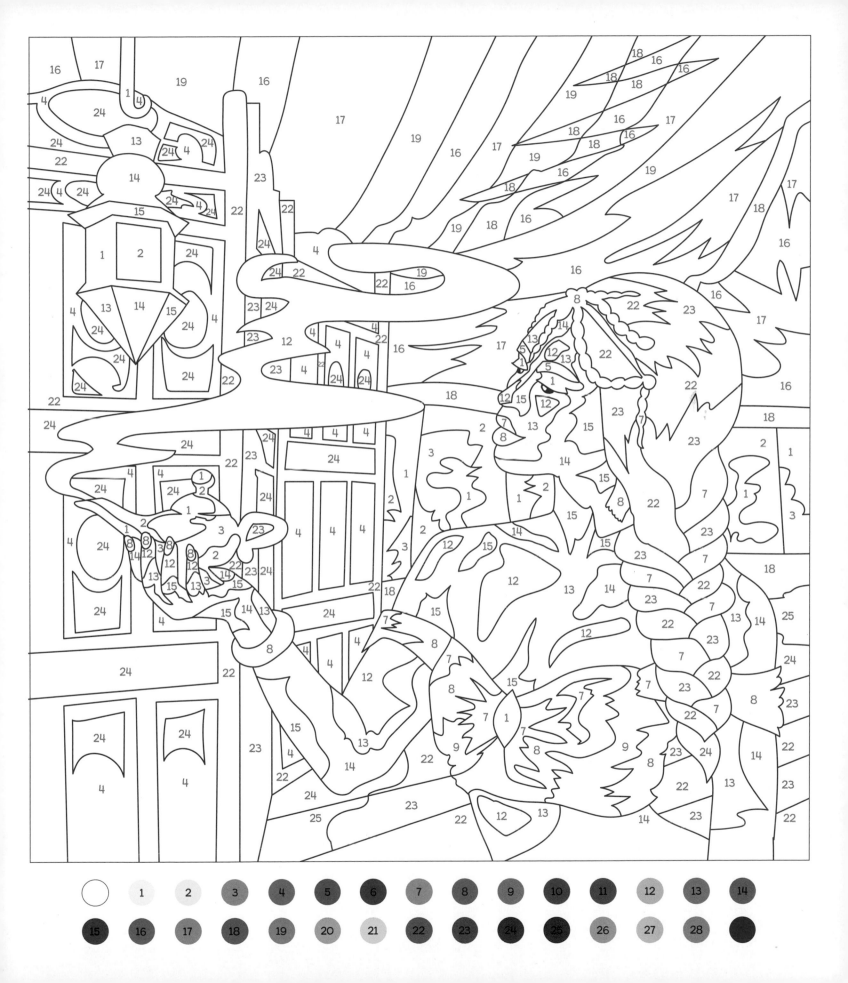

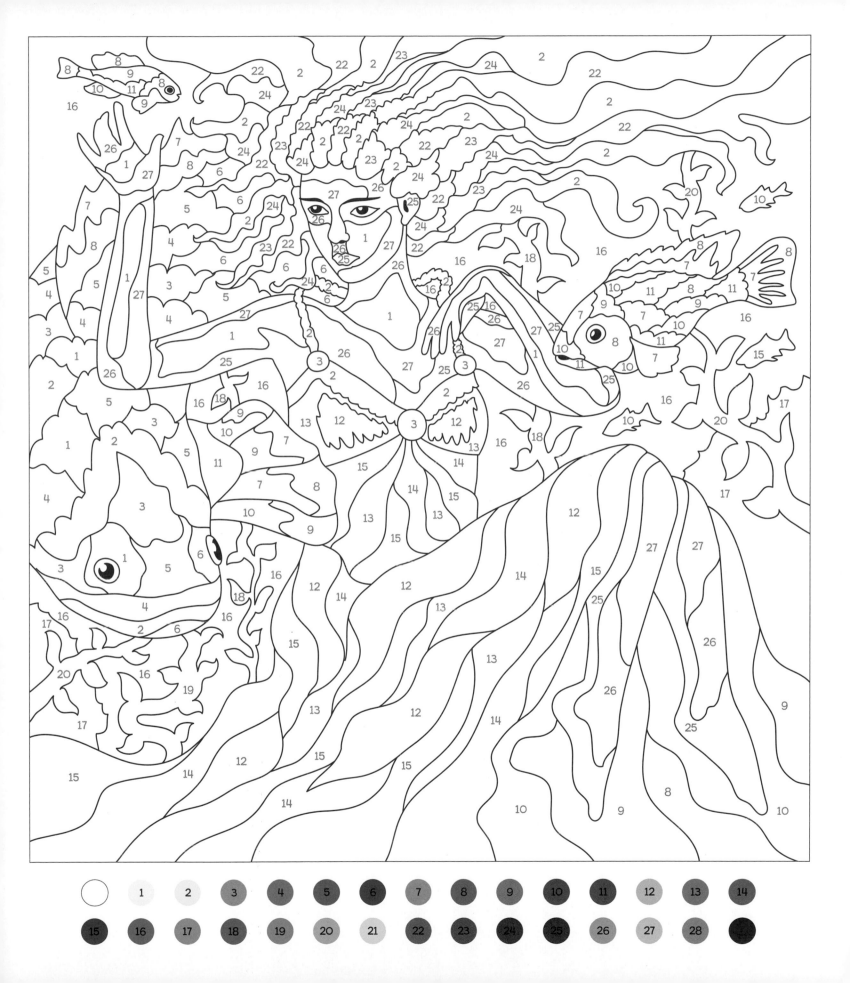

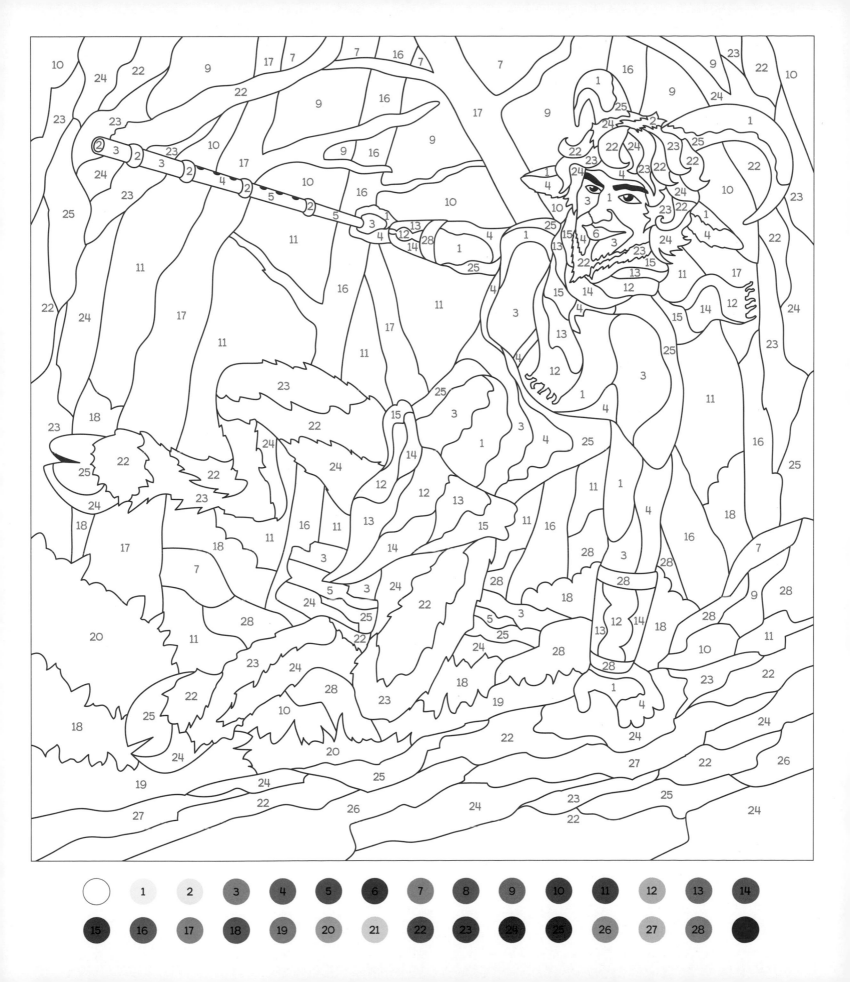

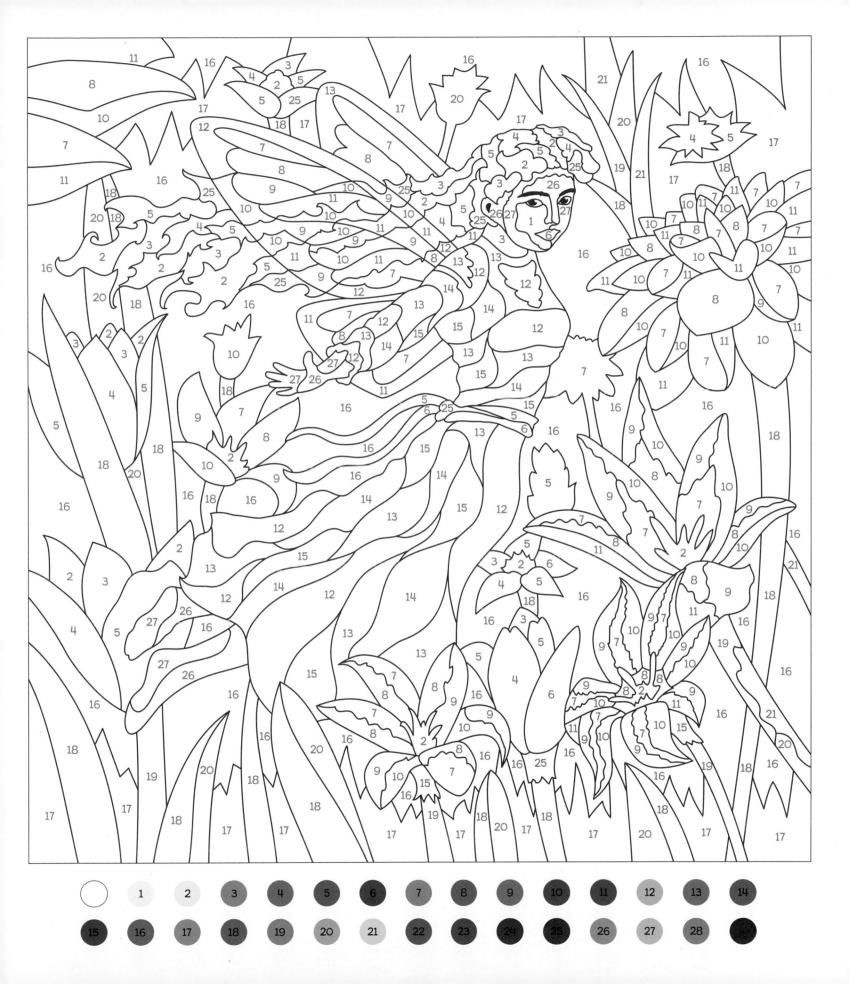

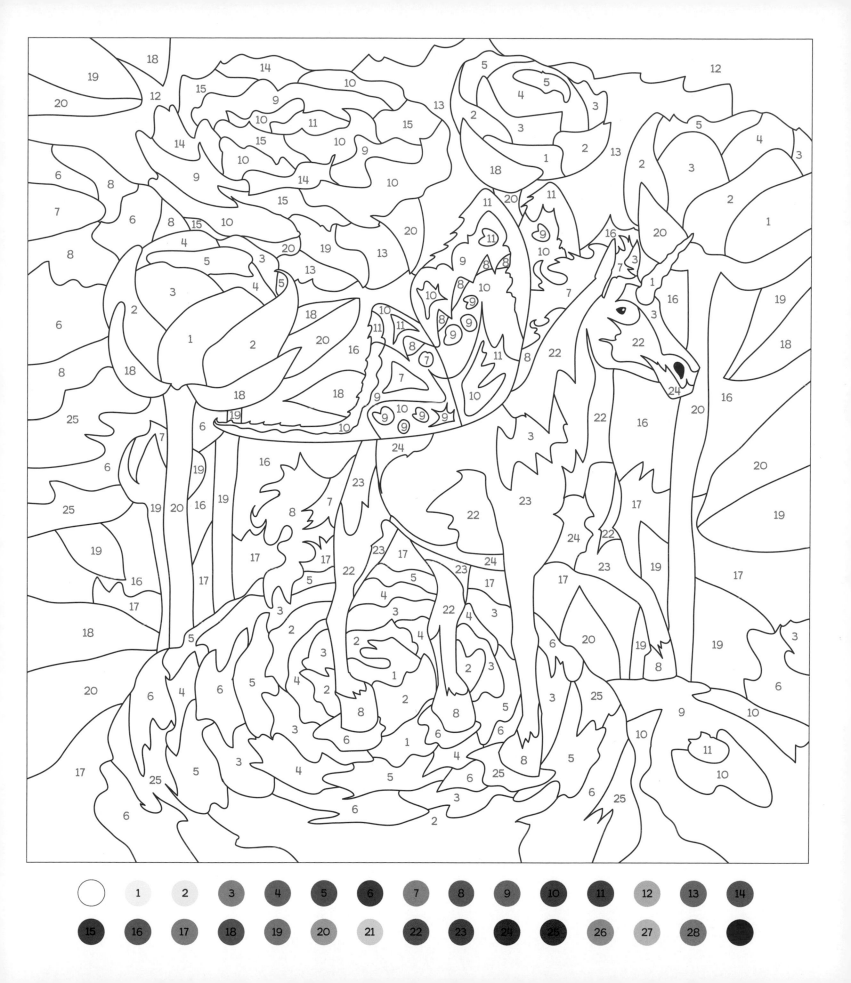

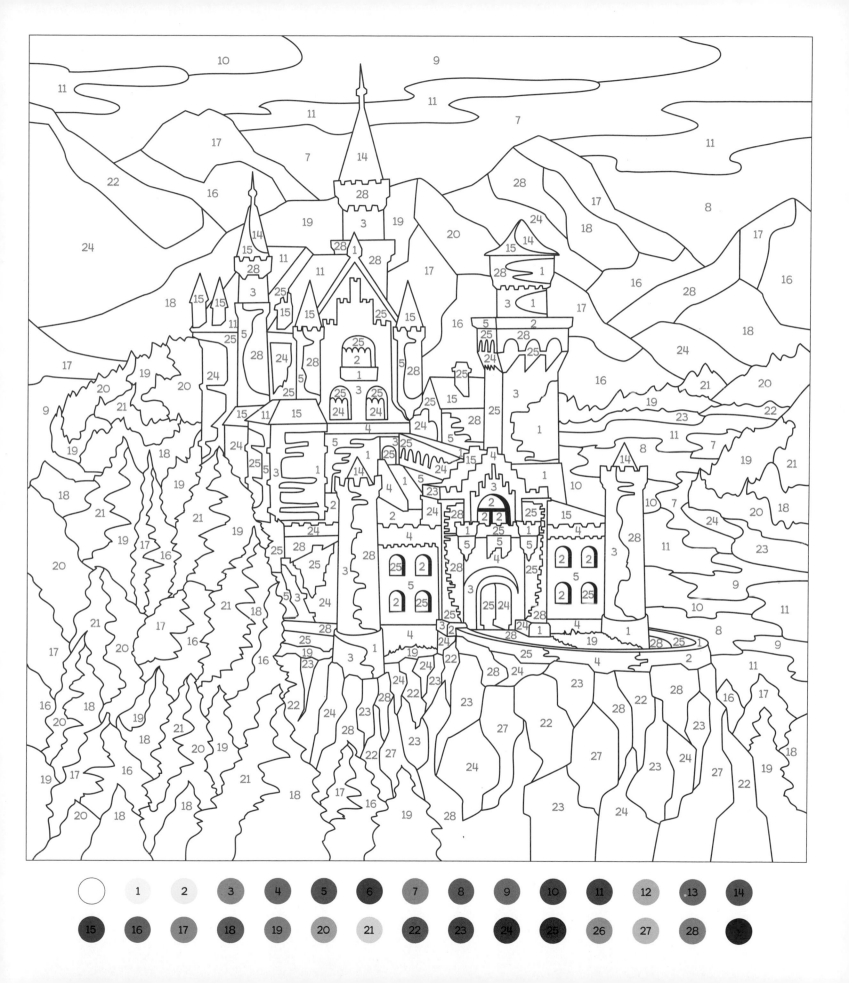

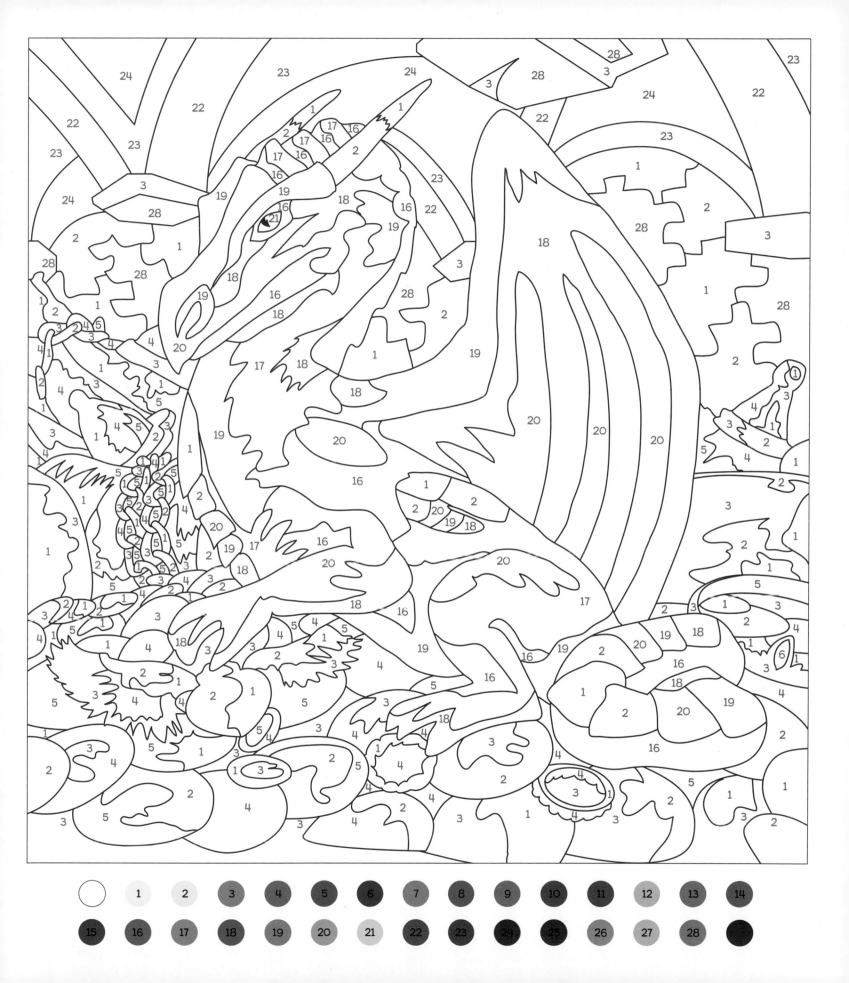

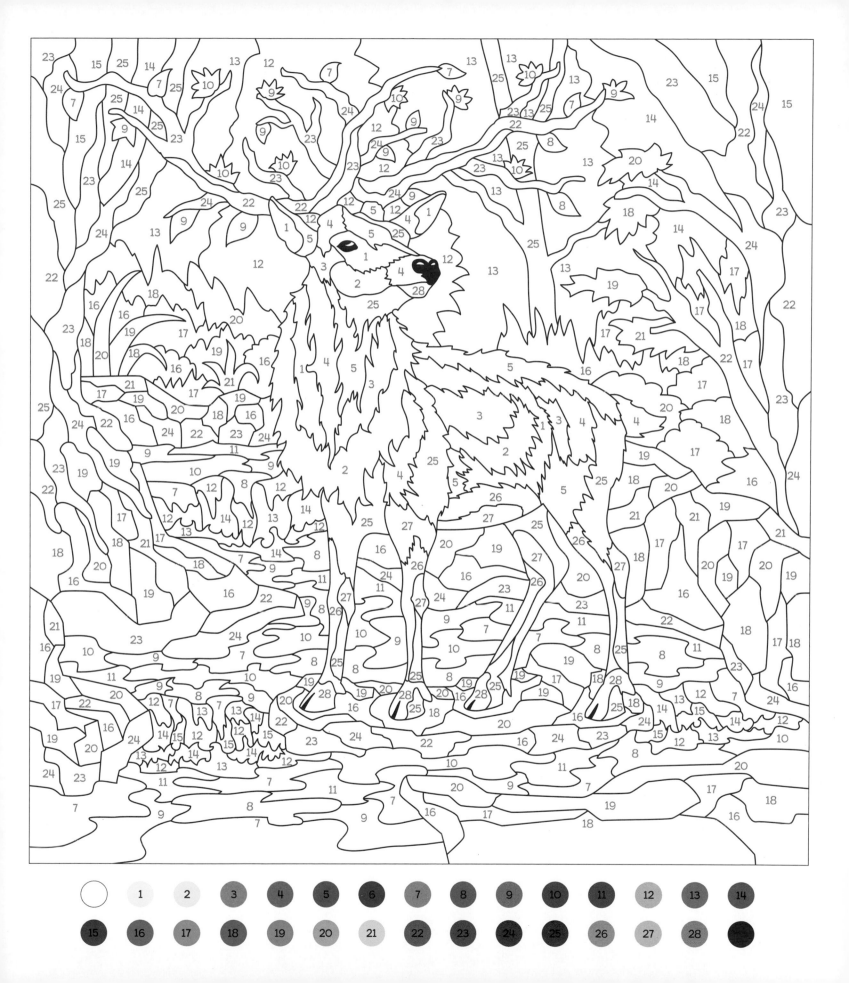

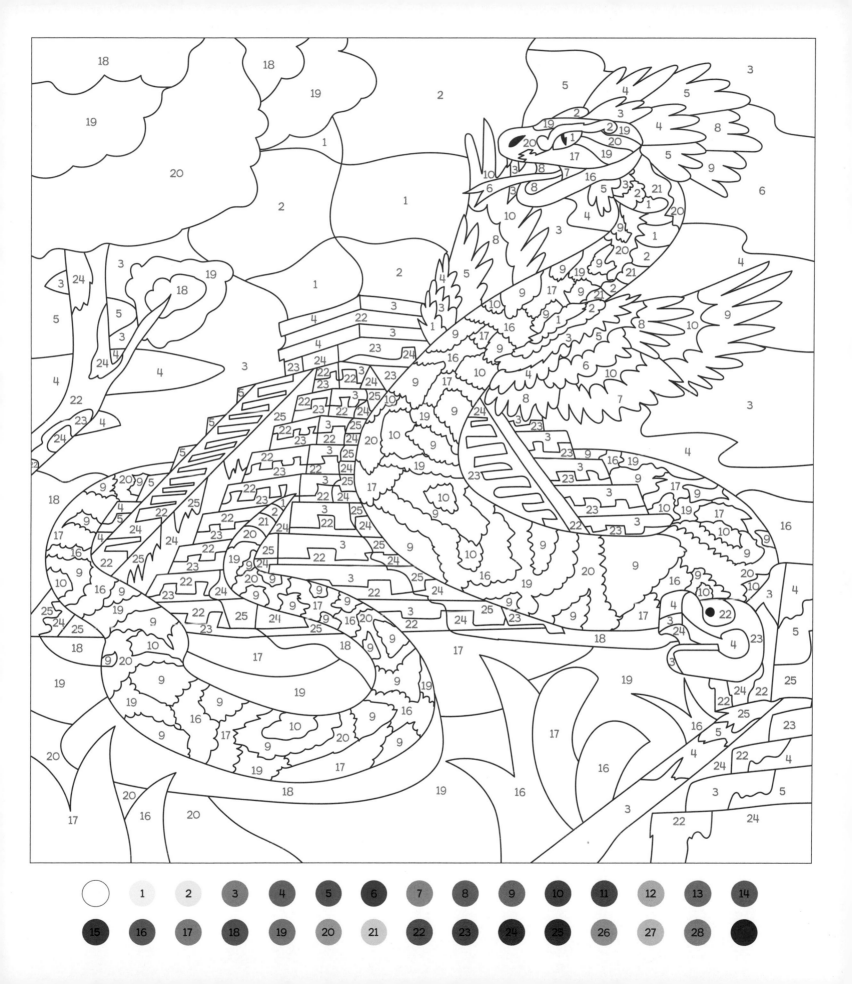

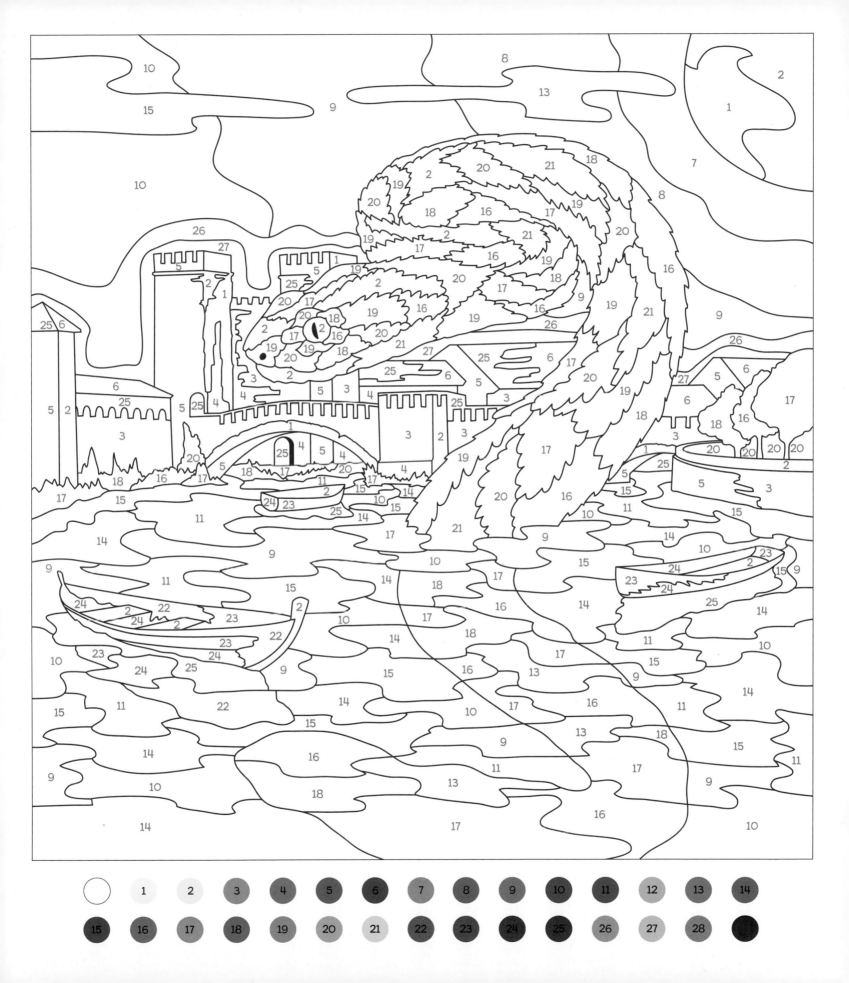

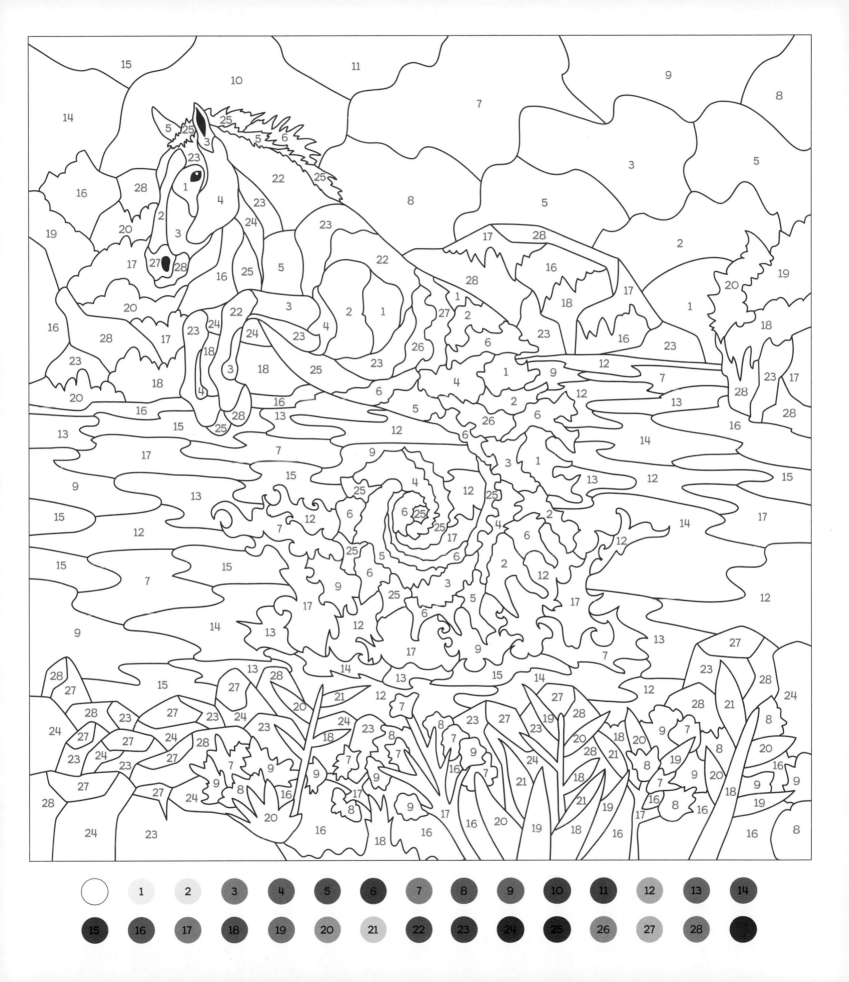

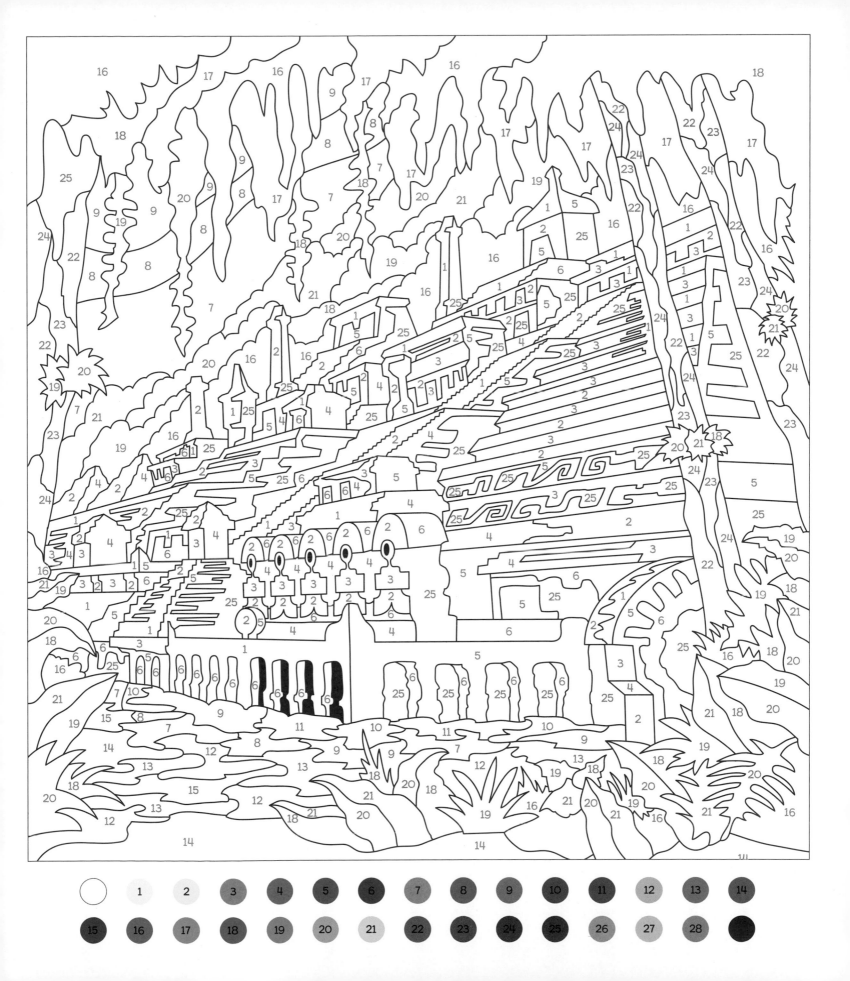

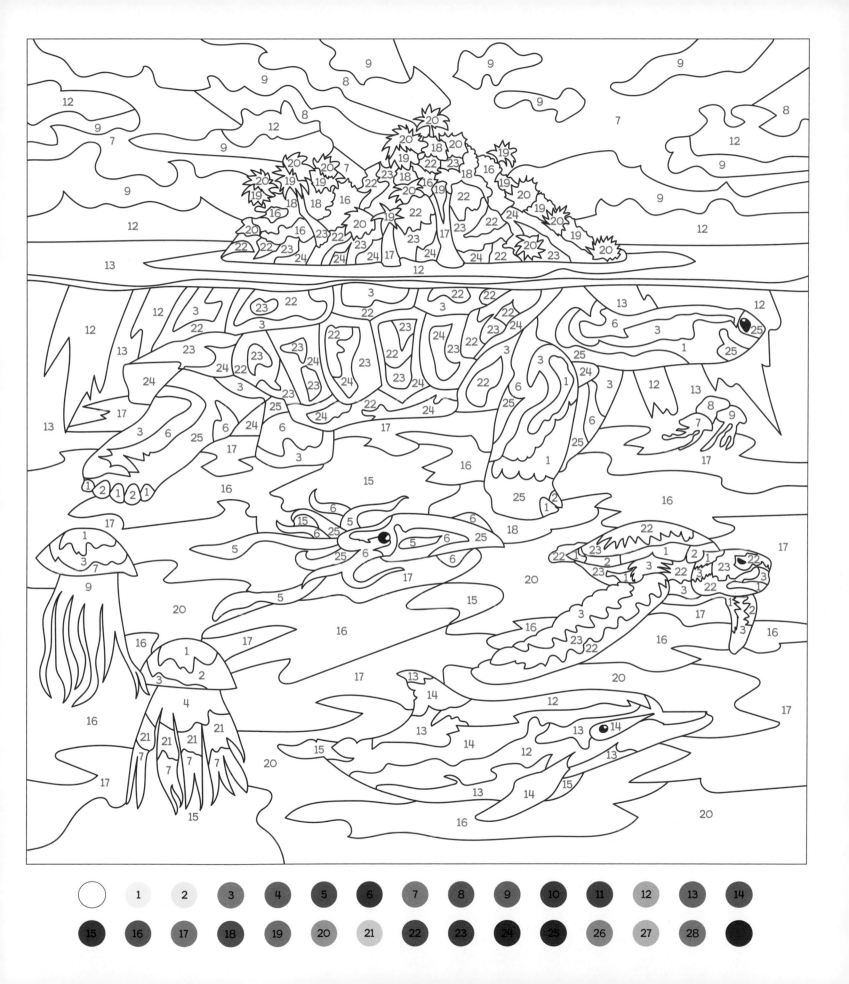

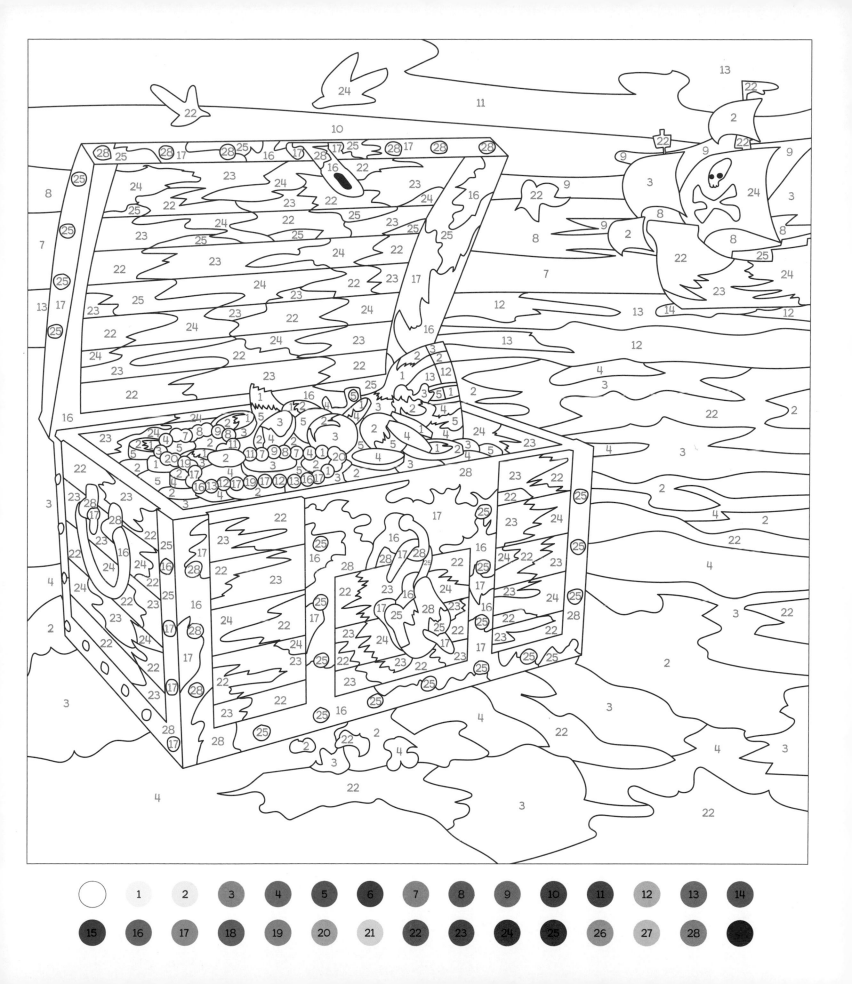

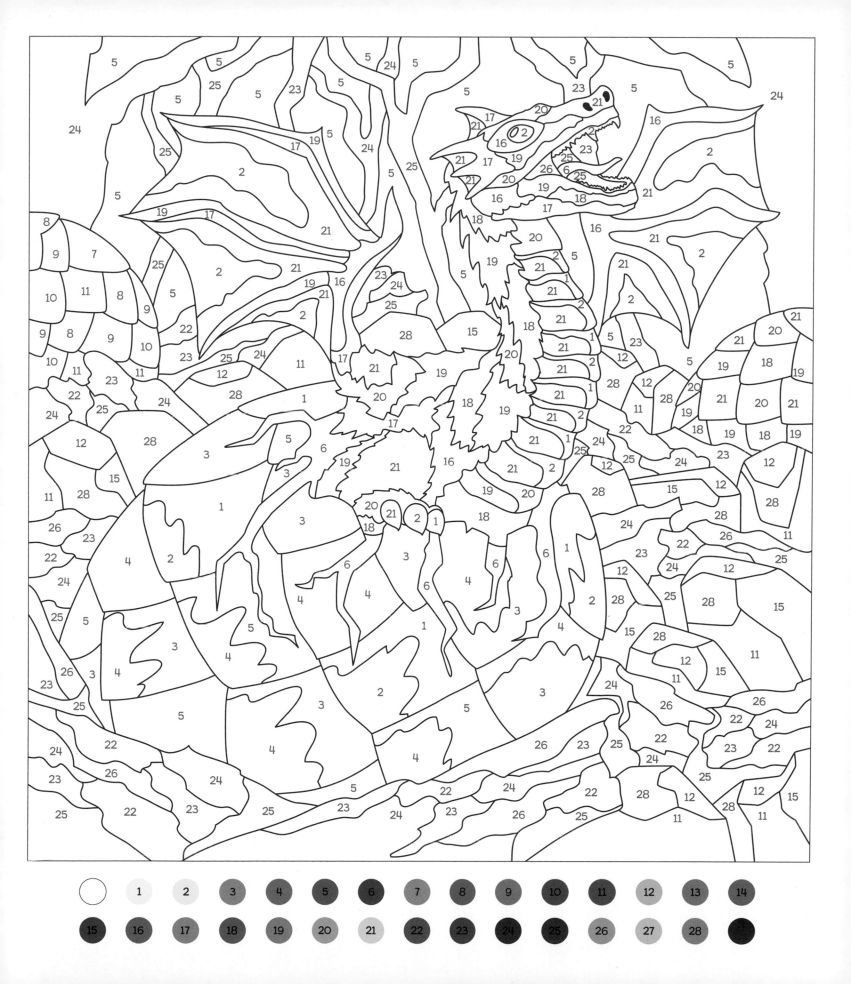

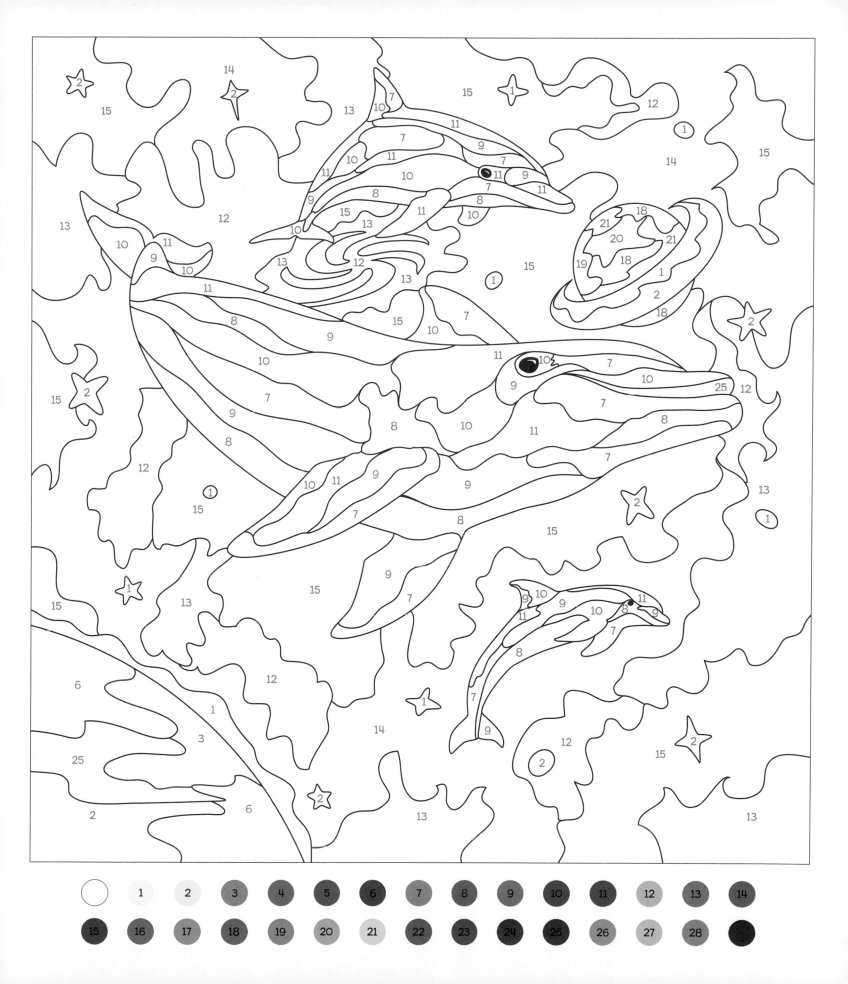

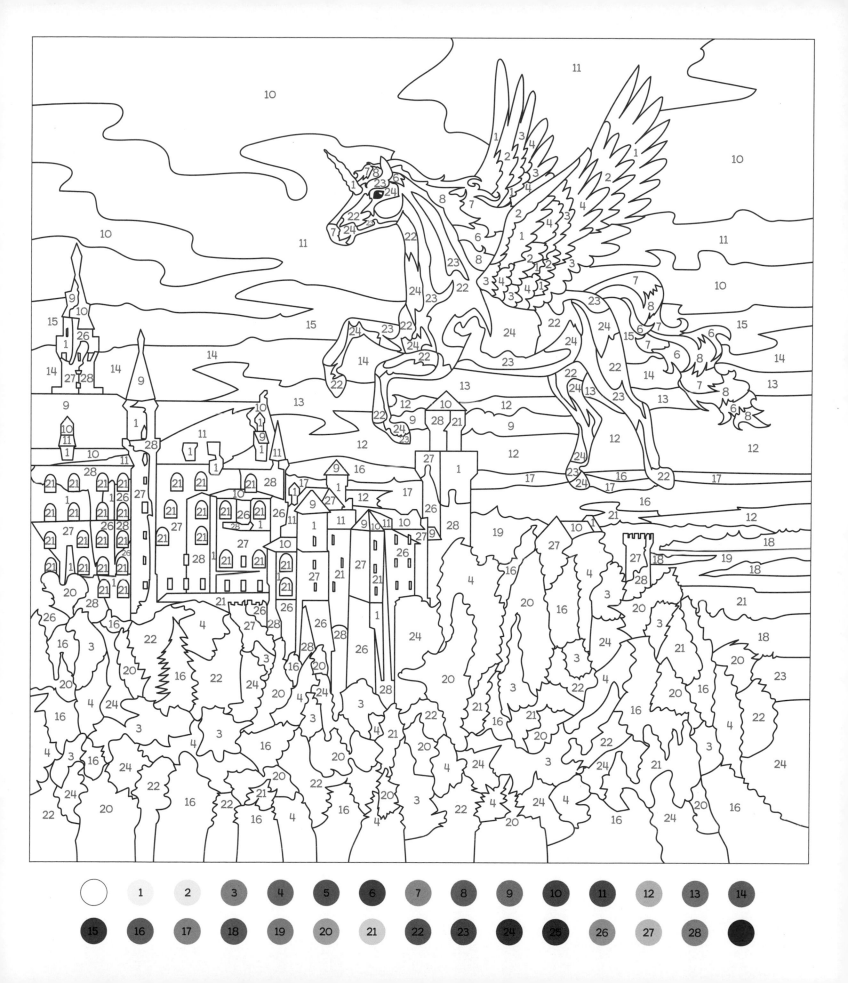

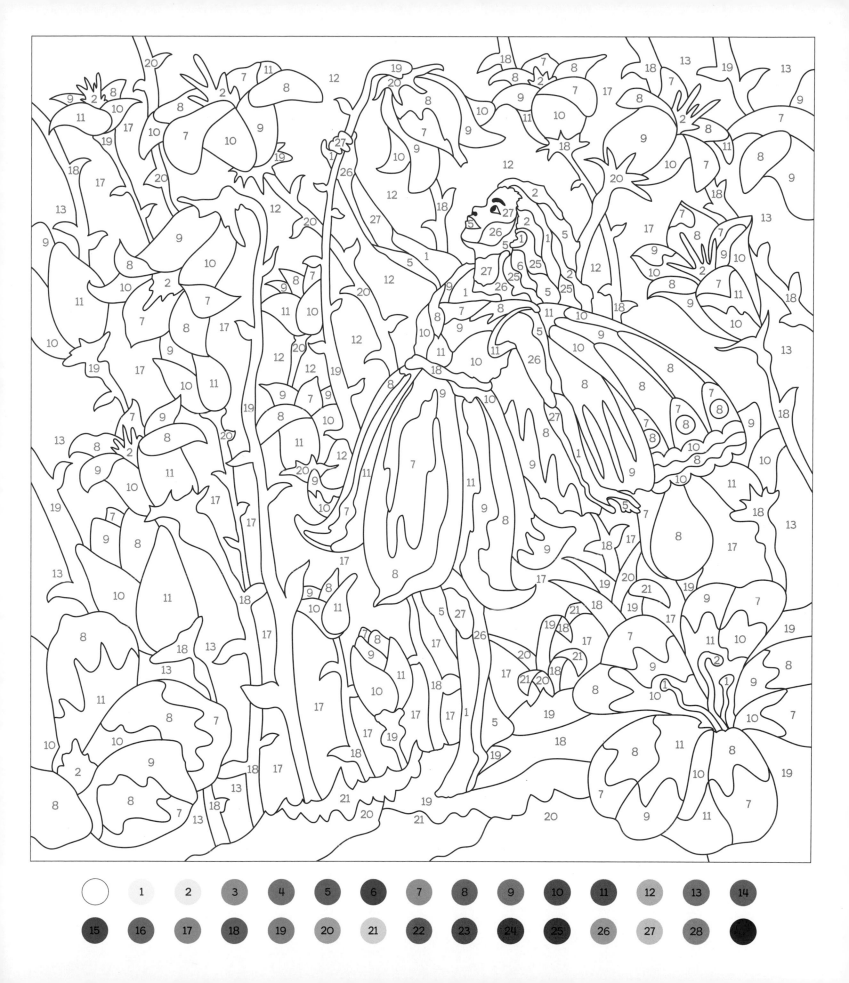

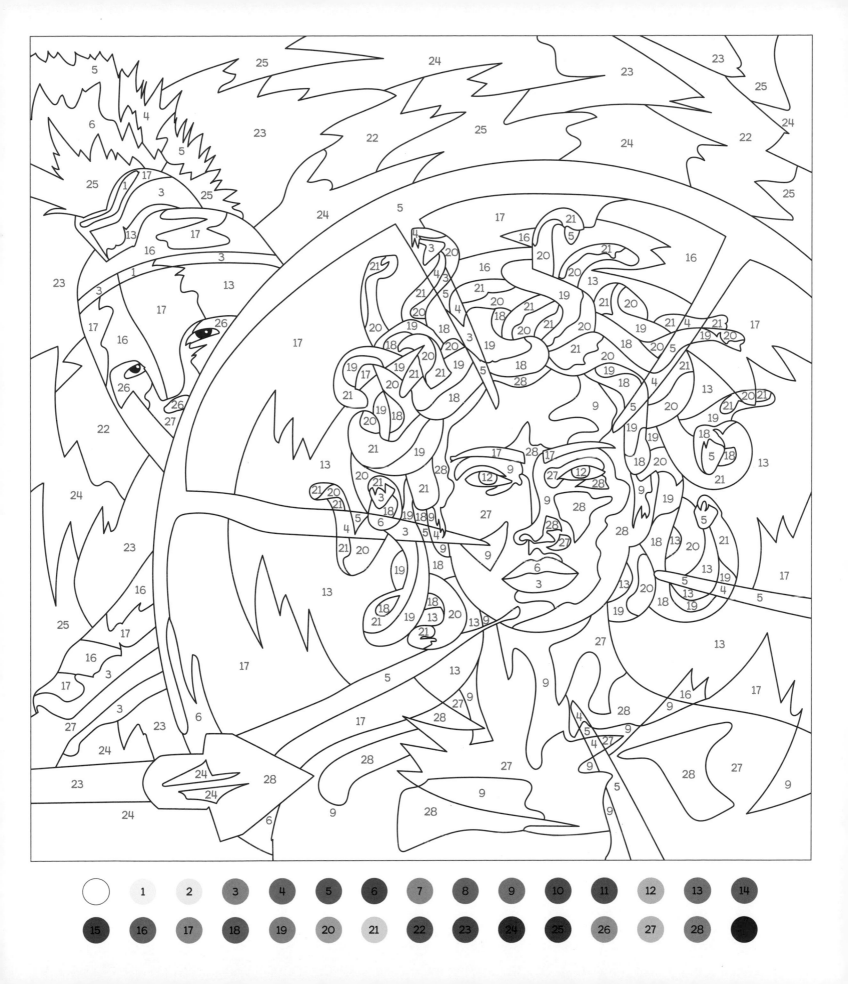

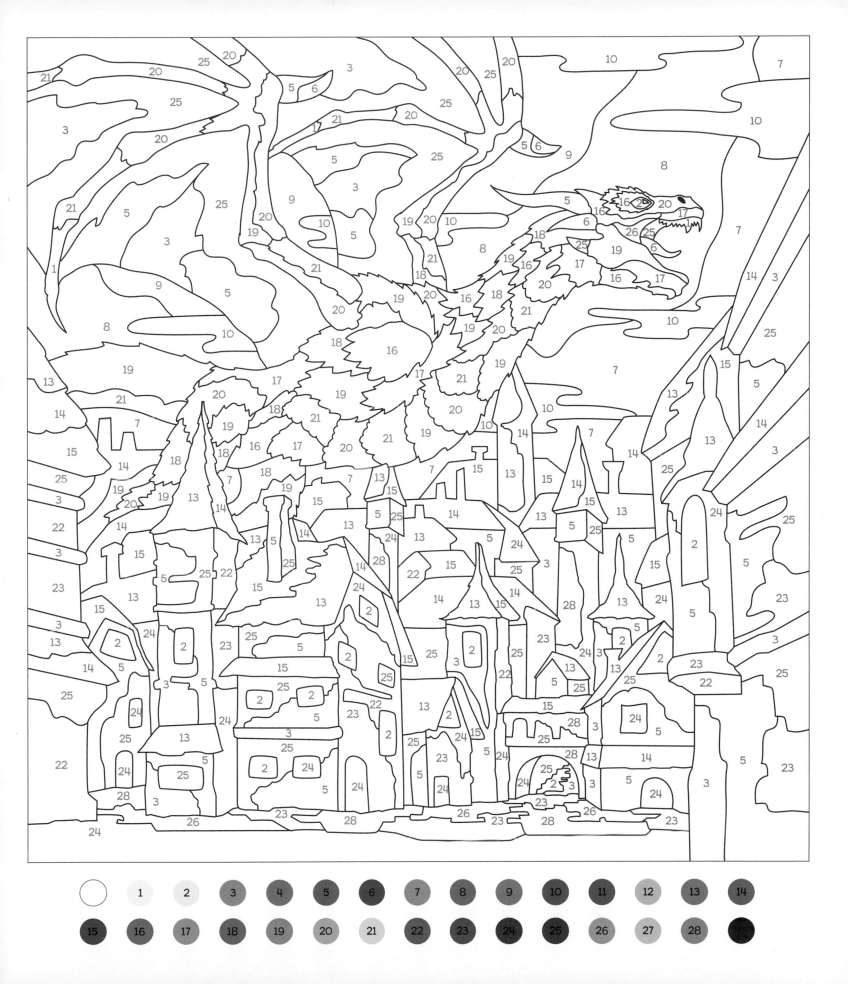

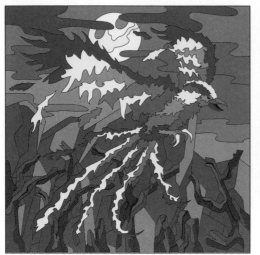

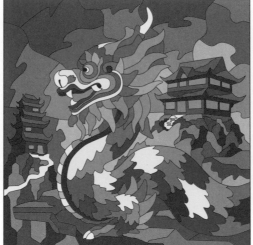

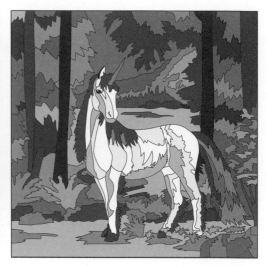

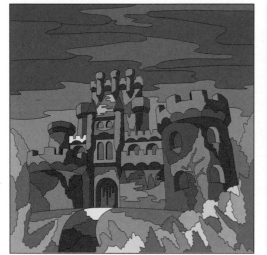

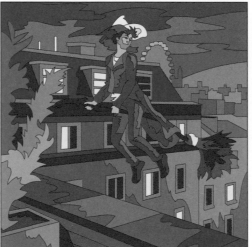

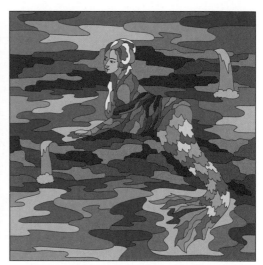

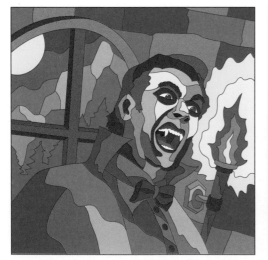

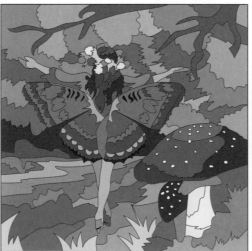

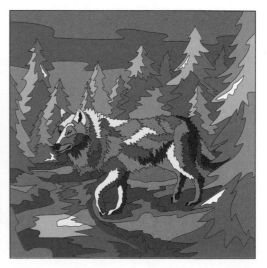

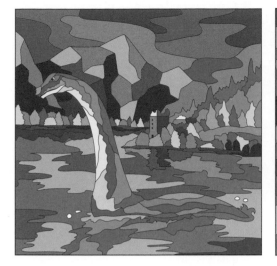

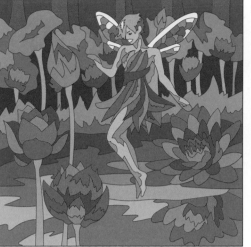

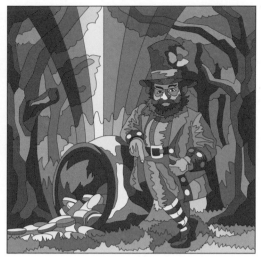

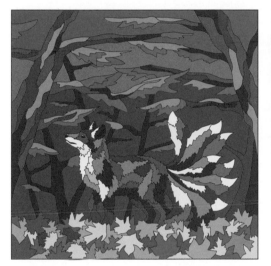

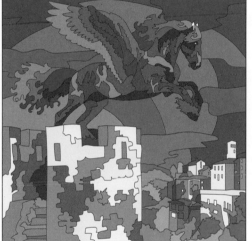

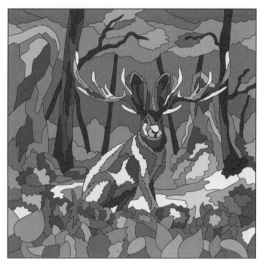

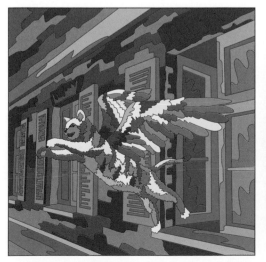

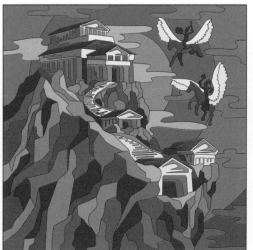

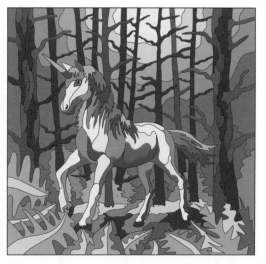

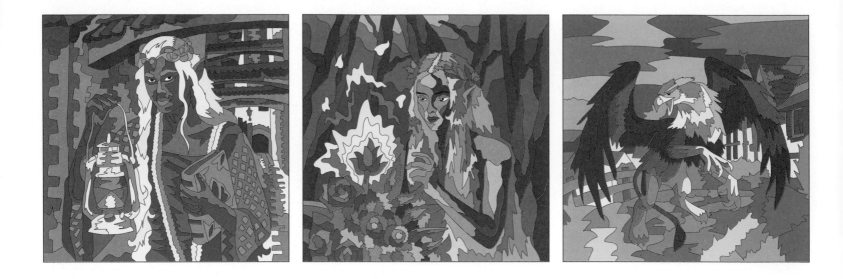

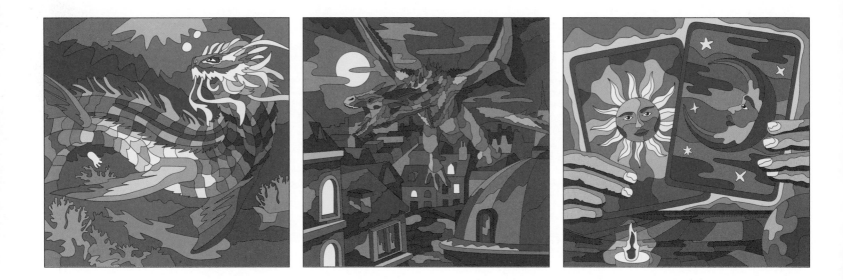

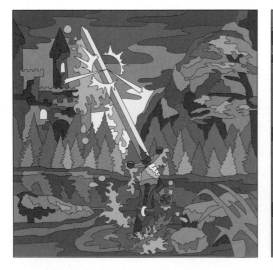
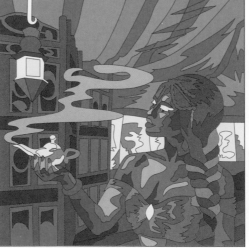
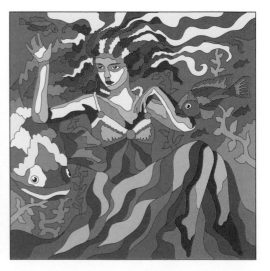

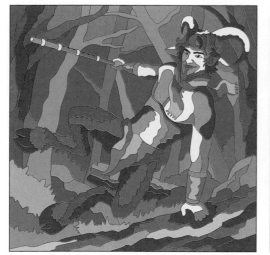 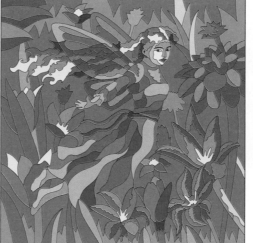 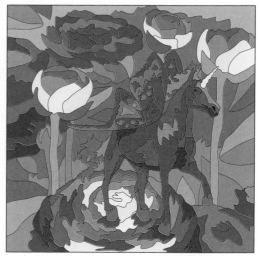

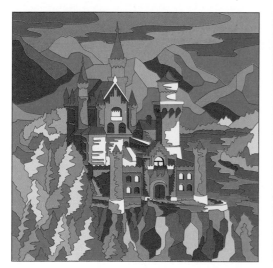 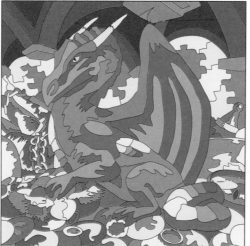 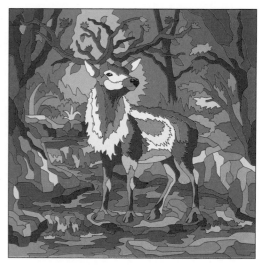

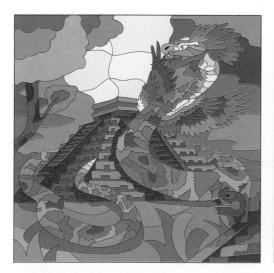 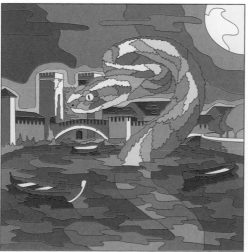 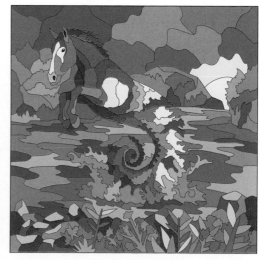

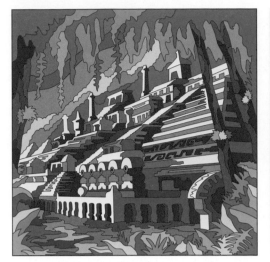
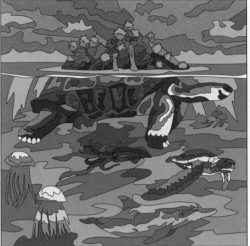
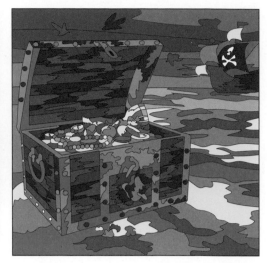
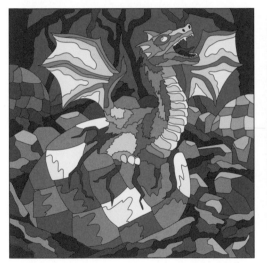
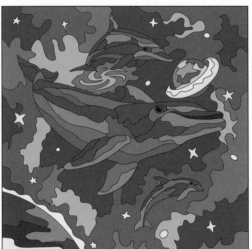
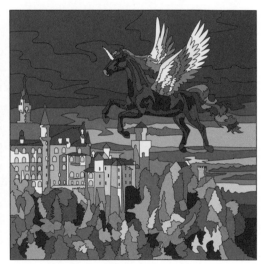
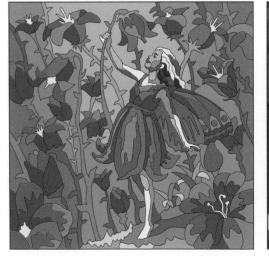
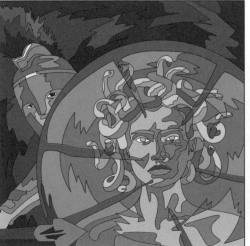
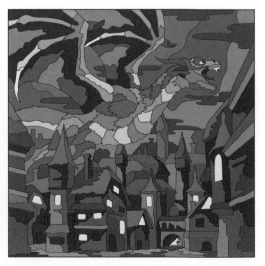